# CHARACTER
# WITNESS

How our lives can make a
difference in evangelism

## Christine Wood

**InterVarsity Press**
Downers Grove, Illinois

InterVarsity Press
P.O. Box 1400, Downers Grove, IL 60515-1426
World Wide Web: www.ivpress.com
E-mail: mail@ivpress.com

InterVarsity Press® is the book-publishing division of InterVarsity Christian Fellowship/USA®, a student
movement active on campus at hundreds of universities, colleges and schools of nursing in the United States
of America, and a member movement of the International Fellowship of Evangelical Students. For
information about local and regional activities, write Public Relations Dept., InterVarsity Christian
Fellowship/USA, 6400 Schroeder Rd., P.O. Box 7895, Madison, WI 53707-7895, or visit the IVCF website
at <www.ivcf.org>.

Cover design: Cindy Kiple

Images: illustration of grapes: Dave Albers/Illustration Works
        red grapes: Linda Holt Ayriss/Artville

ISBN 0-8308-2378-6

Printed in the United States of America ∞

**Library of Congress Cataloging-in-Publication Data**

Wood, Christine, 1943-
    Character witness: how our lives can make a difference in evangelism
/ Christine Wood.
       p. cm.
Includes bibliographical references.
    ISBN 0-8308-2378-6 (pbk.: alk. paper)
    1. Evangelistic work.  I. Title.
    BV3790 .W59 2003
    269'.2—dc 21

                                                                    2002154306

| P | 18 | 17 | 16 | 15 | 14 | 13 | 12 | 11 | 10 | 9 | 8 | 7 | 6 | 5 | 4 | 3 | 2 | 1 |
|---|----|----|----|----|----|----|----|----|----|---|---|---|---|---|---|---|---|---|
| Y | 18 | 17 | 16 | 15 | 14 | 13 | 12 | 11 | 10 | 09 | 08 | 07 | 06 | 05 | 04 | 03 | | |

*This book is dedicated to*

*Lois Dodds,*

*who brought me to Jesus*

*and trained me in his way of life.*

108114

# CONTENTS

# ACKNOWLEDGMENTS

The writing of this book was a team effort. I want to thank my husband, Don, who graciously weathered all of the vicissitudes that came with this project and generously supported me whenever I needed him. Aahmes Overton, Bill Martin and Glenn Ward gave me pastoral support; their theological insights were invaluable to me as I wrote this manuscript. My gratitude for these men, who took time from their full schedules to help me, knows no limit. Cindy Bunch at InterVarsity Press was more than patient in walking me through the writing of this book, my first. My thanks to her for representing Christ to me on every occasion.

I would not be able to work in ministry without the help of a dedicated team. Some of those members lent necessary aid in this project. I appreciate the editorial help I received from Cari Stone, an excellent editor and woman of God who never failed to see my need for encouragement and to give it. Barbara Pine edited this book in its later stages, bringing life and wisdom to its pages. My gratitude to them for their excellent editorial suggestions. My thanks also to Maggie Nelson, who coordinated all the details of this book.

I want to thank all the people I wrote about in this book who have given me permission to tell their stories. You will get the chance to read their stories. Each of them is as wonderful as their stories represent them to be!

# PREFACE

Evangelism. I put a period there because when I mention evangelism, the conversation often stops. Talk of God's goodness, of his gifts to us, of our gratitude for what he grants us—*those* things bring joy. But what of his call to us to make disciples? There, just there, the period is applied. Have you also found that to be true?

Evangelism is a work I have deeply loved for more than thirty years. I confess immediately that my passion for it is like loving to eat strawberries. It seems that God built this love into me.

What if you don't have this feeling about it?

For many of my friends the thought of evangelizing is more like being six years old and sitting before a plate of sliced tomatoes you don't want to eat. Such was the situation my husband, Don, faced. But after graduating from college, he simply became tired of his aversion to tomatoes and decided to discipline himself to eat one tomato each evening in a salad. What do you know—he disciplined himself right into actually liking tomatoes! He noticed that he began to look forward to eating them. He even began putting tomatoes in his sandwiches and eating salads for lunch.

So this book is for those who cringe at the thought of being involved in evangelism. The impetus for finally writing down the stories and experiences found in these pages comes from years of watching God transform lives. I love seeing people melt in their resistance to God, then become eager for him and arrange their lives around his priorities.

## SIMPLE, NOT EASY

I must admit, I also struggle. Evangelism is a paradox—it's simple but not easy. It requires a constant yielding of my time to God's schedule and pace. When I get caught up in my work, I resist the time it takes to be someone's genuine friend. My unbelieving friends challenge my beliefs and threaten any sort of casualness I might slip into concerning the cause of Christ. By their uniqueness they make evangelism a new adventure each time I step onto its path.

Long ago, by a call to authenticity, I was forced to toss aside the various "systems" for rubber-stamping the Spirit of God on the souls of sinners. Evangelism is far more than repetitive phrases or routine; it seems to me to be the communication of holy life through a very ordinary one. It is a human attempt to communicate divine truth. It is a human heart communicating God to another human heart. Who, I wonder, can avoid grappling with the sometimes painful complexities of that?

We glean clues about "how to" from the characteristics that Jesus extended to people he encountered during his three years of ministry—qualities that we, too, can possess. He was intentional, gracious, focused, pure in heart, buoyant, wise, patient, empathetic, reflective, insightful, hospitable, creative and consistent. We will explore these traits through the Scriptures that suggest them.

Imagine these qualities of the Lord as tools in a packet. Last year when I taught in Ecuador, I gave each of my graduate students what I called a survival kit. The class was "designing learning experiences," and my students were teachers already motivated but wanting to improve their skills. In their survival kits were necessary items for class participation: Post-It notes, wide felt pens, a book outlining requirements for the course and instructions for all the learning tasks we would engage in throughout the week. I even included candy to chew on when they needed relief or an extra boost of energy.

At first the students were baffled by some of the items they received. However, by the end of the first hour of class, they discovered for themselves how useful each one was for their learning process. After each unit I taught, the students broke into small groups to apply and analyze the teaching. Within minutes they were writing their insights on the Post-It notes, using the pens so their writing could be seen when they posted their notes on charts to be shared with the whole class. Part of the course was then to apply this method of instructional design to a teaching situation of their own. Now throughout South America, these students are applying creative new methods of teaching.

I offer this book as a survival kit that will give you the basic tools you need to do creative evangelism that fits your style.

## EVANGELISM AND CHARACTER

We're accustomed to thinking about character in terms of morality, and of course, this is crucially important in evangelism. In *Character Witness*, however, I place my focus primarily on relational qualities nearly extinct in our high-tech world. The key to effective evangelism is a relationship that enjoys a pleasing exchange of truth and trust.

Our character usually determines whether or not an unbeliever will risk connection with us. They wonder, *Can I trust Chris? How will she react to my honesty? Will my human problems surprise her? Will she judge me or crawl into my space with compassion?* Most evangelism involves this kind of exchange and this exchange requires relationship. Through my own relational trial and error, I have learned how to become credible enough to non-Christians that they want to hear what I have to say.

I recently attended a secular workshop with my friend Marilyn. In our conversations after the five-day workshop, Marilyn talked about how she and many Christians have some fear, often unconscious, of being harmed by the spiritual beliefs and practices of some non-Christians. This sometimes causes Christians to shy away from involvement with unbelievers.

As we reflected on our conversations with workshop participants who were in the New Age movement, various world religions or simply rejecting "organized religion," Marilyn realized anew regardless of how "confirmed" people seem to be in their beliefs and practices, they will genuinely listen to and respect the sharing of Christians, if they believe that "this is a person worth listening to." Here's where character counts.

Often the initial work of evangelism is damage control. Our first step may be apologizing for hurtful behavior our Christian brothers and sisters have engaged in. I seriously doubt that Christians who endeavor to follow Jesus ever intentionally scar the people they seek to influence. Yet this happens, and when we become aware of it, the words, "I'm so sorry!" speak volumes.

Proficiency in evangelism often doesn't look religious. It's simply treating people as Jesus would treat them.

## TRY IT ON

As you read this book you will have an opportunity at the end of each chapter to "try on" the character quality you have just read about. If you live into this model, you will begin to find yourself receiving invitations from your unbelieving friends to share your ideas and beliefs.

Evangelism is an adventure of becoming the person whose character witnesses to the even deeper reality of who God is and what he offers to those who know the challenges, joys and heartbreaks that define our human lives.

# 1
# INTENTIONAL

## PUTTING CHARACTER
## INTO EVANGELISM

*Preach the gospel at all times. When necessary, use words.*

FRANCIS OF ASSISI

*You are Peter, and on this rock I will build my church.*

MATTHEW 16:18

**INTENTIONALLY** building character means that we resolve to develop Christlike character: that is, we actively engage in putting certain character traits into our lives. In evangelism being intentional means developing relationships with non-Christians.

Who hasn't heard about God? Interstate drivers encounter him on billboards. Messages about him, at nearly any hour, are available via radio and television. He's well represented in bookstores of every sort and is the main subject of sermons preached from countless pulpits every Sunday. Few of us are spared hearing the name of God in conversations, however inappropriately. When tragedy hits, he receives renewed and unprecedented attention and respect, however briefly. Few among us, I am convinced, have not heard about God.

The tragedy is that it appears the essence of God's grace has not penetrated the hearts of those who have heard about him. And the even greater tragedy is that there are more people still looking for God than there are Christians pointing the way.

People almost always understand grace through their own experience. For nearly two years, a woman named Lois brought grace to my life: she lived the gospel before me without using religious words. My understanding of God became real through the experience of her friendship. Lois preaches the gospel through how she treats people.

## INTENTIONAL CHARACTER BUILDING

Character can be understood simply as the collection of identifying marks in one's life. Some characteristics we are born with; some we develop by intention. We can easily see both instances in the apostle Peter. He was naturally impetuous, yet he learned to be reliable. Thank goodness this was so, for Jesus intended that Peter was to be a rock on which he would build his church. Reading New Testament accounts of Peter, we find that he struggled in the years immediately following his conversion. Often he acted without thinking, sometimes with tragic consequences, as when he denied Jesus. He matured as he acknowledged what God had already given him and as he began to intentionally work at Christlike behavior.

Read what he wrote about character, and notice the intentionality involved:

> His divine power has given us everything we need for life and godliness through our knowledge of him who called us by his own glory and goodness. Through these he has given us his very great and precious promises, so that through them you may participate in the divine nature and escape the corruption in the world caused by evil desires.
>
> For this very reason, make every effort to add to your faith goodness; and to goodness, knowledge; and to knowledge, self-control; and to self-control, perseverance; and to perseverance, godliness; and to godliness, brotherly kindness; and to brotherly kindness, love. (2 Pet 1:3-7)

To intentionally develop godly character, a Christian must put forth effort. Unfortunately, the meaning of *intention* has been weakened by our common usage, which implies we are considering an option: "I intend to go on a diet." "I intend to finish school." "I intend to come see you next year."

Years ago, *intended* implied a firm commitment, as did *engagement:* "As soon as Alice became Sam's intended, they set a wedding date and Alice bought her wedding dress." From the moment they became engaged, this couple revealed a firm resolve or solid intention to wed. They went far beyond "considering" marriage.

If we are to evangelize, we must be intentional about developing the kind of character that yields the inviting fragrance of grace. The first step is to begin to understand the people around us.

## OUR CONTEMPORARY RELIGIOUS PROFILE

Despite our fears and misconceptions, the truth is that people today are rarely hostile or belligerent concerning the gospel. They are, and often rightly so, adamantly opposed to being manipulated or demeaned "in Jesus' name." What does it take to engage our culture in conversation about the living God?

In his book *Re-churching the Unchurched,* George Barna describes the American "unchurched" people in the following manner:

18

More than average, these are people who are aggressive, high energy, and driven. They have made something of themselves, by the world's standards. Their hard-charging lifestyle has left many of them frazzled from stress and broken relationships, but they do not necessarily believe that God, Jesus, religion, the Bible, faith or Christianity will help them overcome the struggles they face. They are open to the possibility, but not predisposed to believing that the answer is bound to be faith-based.[1]

It's noteworthy, I think, to consider that the unchurched see Jesus as irrelevant to understanding the complexity of their needs. I fear that in many cases they see Christians as uninformed, dull and, worse still, weak and irrelevant.

George Barna describes five discernable religious segments functioning in America today, which shed light on today's audience for the gospel.[2] Faiths other than Christianity constitute only 7 percent of the population, though that is changing with the growth of Islam. Only 8 percent of our population identify themselves as "atheist or agnostic."

A whopping 85 percent of Americans identify themselves as "Christian," and these can be further divided into three distinct groups. Forty-four percent of them are, according to Barna, "notional Christians": a group of 90 million Americans who consider themselves Christians but don't embrace core biblical doctrines. They often went to church as children, yet only a minority still attend. Few view the Bible as authoritative or see commitment to the Christian faith as important.

Thirty-three percent believe they have eternal life through Jesus, but even though the majority of them attend church, they are likely to consult sources other than the Bible or religious literature regarding questions of morality. While they read the Bible and pray during the week, these activities make little appreciable difference in their choices of behavior. Many of these people need our influence.

Obviously when we think of evangelism today, we must include in our audience some people who identify themselves as Christians. If the 77 percent identified in the above two groups are to become Christian disciples—transformed by Jesus to a new way of thinking, feeling and behaving—they need a new sense of his relevance in daily life.

Of the original 85 percent of Americans who identify themselves as Christians, only 8 percent describe themselves as being evangelical: that is, they believe their relationship with Jesus Christ will lead to eternal life. Three out of four self-described evangelicals shared their faith with an unbeliever during the year. People in this group are likely to base their moral decisions on the Bible. They are the most active in religious endeavors like reading the Bible and going to church; and a majority of this group will be found in conservative, evangelical churches. Because those of us in this group are a minority in America, we often feel isolated and insignificant as we stand outside of mainstream society.

In my experience the evangelical group is least likely to understand broad human issues or to deal with them compassionately. We are apt to overspiritualize problems. We don't want to spend time listening to unbelievers talk about their problems because we think it is more Christian to preach than to listen. If any of us among this 8 percent (the very 8 percent that may well care most passionately about genuine faith) want to engage in effective evangelism, we will need to be intentional in how we live our lives and act toward nonbelievers. *Intentionality in evangelism means that Christians actively pursue their own personal growth (that is, maturity in Christ) and that they engage non-Christians in an open, ongoing dialogue about the role Jesus plays in this process.* In this context we make Christ relevant to our unbelieving friends.

## INTENTIONAL EVANGELISM IN PRACTICE

I was among the other 8 percent: those identified by Barna as agnostic and unchurched. I came to know Jesus after two years of receiving tender and unconditional love from my friend Lois. She personified intentional evangelism, and her influence still continues to shape my life. Interestingly, it was in the way she lived, not in the words she said, that she initially shared Christ with me. This busy woman took the time to hang out with me.

We met and became friends as classmates at our local junior college. We grappled with the ideas presented in a course we took together. We agreed on very little. I found secular atheistic writers to be of great comfort; Lois found them depressing. I agreed with Albert Camus's conviction that suicide was a valid option; Lois remained more optimistic. I was a liberal, articulate young woman; Lois was a conservative—though equally articulate—Christian woman who wasn't afraid of rigorous mental exercises. I could tell she was a Christian, and I tolerated it because our conversations were so stimulating. I also observed intriguing characteristics in Lois that were altogether unfamiliar and curiously winsome.

We were living in tumultuous times. Given the personal suffering I carried inside of me—to which was added the deep heartache of living through the assassinations of John and Robert Kennedy and Martin Luther King Jr., and the unending confusion of the Vietnam War with its seemingly senseless casualties—I felt my morbid conclusions validated. Lois chose a higher road.

I was equally impressed with Lois's attitude toward everyday life. She came to my house for coffee, and when she slipped into the bathroom to change her infant's diaper, she sang! With two baby boys of my own, I had plenty of distraction tactics up my sleeve, but believe me, singing wasn't one of them. Often, Lois's kind response to unpleasant situations and daily hassles arrested my attention.

Intuitively, I knew she was different from me on the inside. Watching her, I craved the freedom and lightheartedness she exuded. For almost two years no words about these observations passed between us. I continued to be my liberated self, and Lois listened to what I had to say. We grappled with life together. Unknown to me at the time, Lois turned her insights from our conversations into prayers for me. The insights came from her understanding of God and Scripture and from dealing with her own issues. Yes, I was confused, even desperate at times, but Lois knew I was far too hostile to hear the gospel yet. Wisely, she lived a consistent life, listened, prayed and waited. She hoped I would become a Christian. Though I appeared capable and confident, Lois knew I needed Jesus. Her intention was to model his grace to me in every opportunity.

Often during this time she called for no reason other than to ask how I was doing. She'd make contact simply because she wanted to talk to me. She had no agenda, just a listening, compassionate ear. Lois intended to be a good friend. Her actions disarmed me. Here was a full-time student and mother of three young children calling to see how I was. Not even members of my own family did that!

I'd grown up with high-achieving relatives and parents whose lives were controlled and eventually ruined by alcohol abuse. At the time I met Lois, I had a recurring image of myself splattered against a freeway wall—my blood dripping and sinking into thirsty concrete and leaving an indelible stain. To be honest, I had concluded that such feelings were normal and not worth mentioning. I carried that nightmare inside me all the time: through all my successes at school and in the community, during each stimulating discussion with Lois on existentialism and even while playing at the beach with my children.

As our friendship developed I learned that Lois lugged some baggage of her own. She was one of twelve children, reared by a devout mother and an enigmatic father. Although a self-proclaimed missionary, he was a failure as a husband and a parent. Lois's mother tried to stand in the gap created by his inconsistencies. However, with twelve children to care for, she was limited in what she could do. Sadly, the profile of Lois's siblings reads like a social worker's worst caseload: jail, prison, cynicism, hostility, divorce, suicide and rejected faith.

Lois certainly wasn't left emotionally unscathed. Yet there she was, the antithesis to her father's hypocrisy and her mother's defeat. Lois had room in her soul for her family, for me and for countless others. Lois knew what the apostle Peter knew—that to respond to the call of Jesus, one must intentionally develop a godly disposition. When she was overwhelmed, she prayed, and it seemed that God provided what she needed to go forward in peace. When she was tired after a long day at school, she remained patient and kind to her children. When someone was unkind, she was charitable. The more I witnessed her behavior, the more I wanted to understand its source. The qualities I observed in Lois were not at all like those I'd observed in other professing Christians.

Ironically, her relationship with me caused some concern among her well-meaning church friends. They cautiously questioned her, asking why she pursued a friendship with someone who they felt sure would never become a Christian. Their intention was to avoid me. I thank God that Lois saw well beyond the presuppositions of her church friends and straight into my heart. She enjoyed our relationship and felt my need for compassion and love.

The world is full of people who are filled with bitterness, just as I was. These are capable individuals, many of whom have achieved outward success. Despite my inner turmoil, I was still able to handle my family responsibilities, start a Montessori school and attend college.

Another example of such a capable person is Lance Armstrong, the United States' brightest hero in the world of professional cycling. In the late 1990s he wrestled with metastasized, third-stage testicular cancer and won. He went on to conquer the most grueling endurance road race of its kind, the Tour de France, and won that too—in 2002 for the fourth time. To these achievements add an incredible home life with a beautiful wife and children whose births, in light of Lance's illness, were nothing short of miraculous.

Armstrong is a genuine, remarkable guy. He has endured unbelievable hardships, overcome odds and committed himself to discipline and right relationships with the people in his life. Yet his reflections on personal theology reflect the influence of postmodern, secular thought.

I wished hard, but I didn't pray. I had developed a certain distrust of organized religion growing up, but I felt I had the capacity to be a spiritual person, and to hold some fervent beliefs. Quite simply, I believed I had a responsibility to be a good person, and that meant fair, honest, hardworking, and honorable. If I did that, if I was good to my family, true to my friends, if I gave back to my community or to some cause, if I wasn't a liar, a cheat, or a thief, then I believed that should be enough. At the end of the day, if there was indeed some Body or presence standing there to judge me, I hoped I would be judged on whether I had lived a true life, not on whether I believed in a certain book, or whether I'd been baptized. If there was indeed a God at the end of my days, I hoped he didn't say, "But you were never a Christian, so you're going the other way from heaven." If so, I was going to reply, "You know what? You're right. Fine."[3]

One thing I know from my interactions with high-achieving people like this (and from having to some degree been one myself) is that, like it or not, notice it or not, somewhere deep inside each of us is a hole that only God can fill. If we as Christians are willing to be intentional about evangelizing the people God places within our sphere of influence, he will give us the tools we need to be unconditional, trusted friends to them. He will help us shape the kind of characteristics that are both observable and appealing to our unbelieving friends. One day they may invite us to talk about God, as I did one day with Lois. When this happens God will give us the words that offer them life.

How do we become trusted by the nonbelievers God places in our lives? How do we earn either the invitation or the right to speak into their lives? We must develop an attractive character. If we are winsome, people *want* to be with us. Over time they are apt to inquire about what makes us think, feel and act as we do. In a culture saturated with impersonal contacts and contrived communication, winsomeness is a natural and appealing invitation to relationship. By being intentional we can develop the qualities needed for an engaging character. In this atmosphere, evangelism occurs.

For years I've kept a personal journal. I have also attended various journal seminars, where I've met people from around the world. At these seminars, participants share their journals with each other, revealing their very souls. These interactions and my own life experiences together confirm for me three foundational truths.

*Almost every adult is willing to be known once he or she feels safe.* As Christians, we must create a safe place for people whose paths we cross. We need to stand in the confidence of Christ, demonstrating patience and a positive, unconditional love to those who don't yet know him. Unbelievers simply don't feel safe with a person who barges into their lives without first establishing genuine respect and rapport.

*Many adults bury the emotions that accompany pain and sin, unaware that good can be found in that terrible internal mix.* In our relating to them it is imperative that we find the good in their lives and build on it. This means that we must take seriously God's statement in Genesis 1:26: "Let us make man in our image, in our likeness." As we reach out to those who don't yet know Christ as their Lord and Savior, we need to remind ourselves that we are interacting with people who are created in God's image. We must show them the respect they deserve. We must pray for God's view of their hearts rather than relate to how they appear on the surface. This doesn't mean that we ignore sin. Sooner or later issues of sin will surface, and the consequences of sin will be confronted.

The field of education offers a principle of sequence that applies here: "If you want to teach someone how to swim, don't start at the deep end of the pool." Many unbelievers have turned away from Christianity because overly eager evangelists threw them into deep water before teaching them to swim.

*Healthy adults know the importance of being heard and making their own choices.* Most people I've observed—whether Muslim, Jewish, Hindu, Christian, theist, agnostic or atheist—respond to the pressure of strictly imposed conformity by clamming up or rejecting such demands. We are each created with the freedom to choose for ourselves, in our own time and in our own way; and while we may encourage others to choose a certain way, we are never free to force them.

As Christians, we participate with God in his call to unbelievers by reflecting his character to them. We must also remember that it is God who changes hearts. Coercion and manipulation don't work in evangelism. Thankfully we can look to Jesus for leadership in this. At appropriate moments he exhibited a bold and forthright attitude; his conversations with the Sadducees and Pharisees provide excellent examples. In other circumstances he wisely chose a calm and quiet approach. Always his actions were prompted by the Holy Spirit and were appropriate to the situation.

Humanly speaking, it's difficult if not impossible to change the beliefs of the people Barna profiled. Quite frankly, we miss the mark completely if our attempts stem from our own agendas. The work of evangelism proves all the more challenging until we abandon our own devices. The collection of people we may influence to faith are as diverse as the rubber bands found in a package I recently purchased: multicolored and varied in every way. Here is one narrow of attitude, another wide in kindness; others are small-job capable, large-job powerful, blue-collar, white-collar, no-collar, rich, poor, immigrant or native born. Jesus, too, lived in a cultural free-for-all. Romans, Greeks, Samaritans, Gentiles and Jews shared a small space and shared a large need for God. We are prepared to represent the Lord when we remember that Christ's authority—that authority we possess through the Great Commission—is empowered by the will of God, not our own. What a liberating realization.

## PRINCIPLES OF ENGAGEMENT

If the 8 percent of Christians who take Scripture seriously were to engage in winsome evangelism, we could surely influence our culture. I'm talking about the kind of commitment that will change our lives, our churches and the people in our world. We will begin by focusing on what we can do, not what we cannot. Here are some recommendations to help you get started.

First, I urge you to move through this book slowly, say, a chapter a week. For example, this week you can mull over what it would take for you to be intentional about evangelism. You can do this by working through the "Engage in Becoming Intentional" section below.

If adults are going to learn something, they have to be actively engaged in it. *We learn by doing,* so if you do the exercises I've provided, you will learn how to be evangelistic. I suggest that you mark pages when you come to something useful in each chapter. Then work through the exercises. Their purpose is to get you moving toward living out the characteristic focused on in each chapter. You may find yourself adding insights as you consider them for a few days.

It would be advantageous for you to then meet with a small group to talk about what you are discovering and doing. Adults learn best what they discover for themselves and what they discuss with their peers. You will be learning a lot about yourself and others as you engage with this material. (I've included an appendix for small-group leaders that you will find helpful in leading a group.)

---

## ENGAGE IN BECOMING INTENTIONAL

---

1. What in this chapter is useful to you? Why do you think this is so?

2. Consider the person who led you to Christ. What character qualities marked that person and made him or her winsome to you?

3. In Acts 13:4-13 we find Paul's first recorded experience of evangelism on his first missionary journey. Read this text aloud, slowly. Imagine yourself as Paul, and look for ways he demonstrated intentionality.

   a. How was God's call to Paul evident?

   b. Had you been Paul, what might you have thought and felt before embarking on this first missionary journey?

c. What difference might it make if a believer were to actively seek God's help in being intentional in evangelism through worship, prayer and fasting?

d. What behaviors showed Paul's intentionality?

e. What purpose did the blinding of the magician serve for both Elymas and the proconsul? How might that insight help you in evangelism?

f. How does John reveal a lack of being intentional? Comment on what you think he missed.

4. Make a list of the *places* where you have opportunity to be with people who don't yet share your Christian faith. (Consider, for example, where you spend your time and money as well as your interests and hobbies.)

5. Name some *people* in these places who seem to respond well to you or for whom you have a particular burden. Pray for these people, and then choose two or three whom you would most like to influence for Christ.

6. Specify what you would need to do or change to be intentional in evangelizing these people.

# 2

# GRACIOUS

## WHERE HUMAN MEETS THE DIVINE

*Man is born broken; he lives by mending. The Grace of God is the glue.*

EUGENE O'NEILL

*The Word became flesh and made his dwelling among us. We have seen his glory, the*
*glory of the One and Only, who came from the Father, full of grace and truth. . . .*
*From the fullness of his grace we have all received one blessing after another. For the*
*law was given through Moses; grace and truth came through Jesus Christ.*

JOHN 1:14, 16-17

BEING GRACIOUS stems from having our
lives and relationships with others marked by
God's grace—his steadfast, unconditional love. In
evangelism, this means that our thoughts, emotions and behavior toward non-Christians are
marked by graciousness as we seek to bring them
to Jesus and commit to serve him as King.

I magine being a child who possesses a keen sense of beauty and order but lives in a dirty home, soiled by piles of animal waste, covered by layers of dust and endless clutter. Imagine, in this mess, that it is dinnertime. Four children scramble for a place at the table. The parents, well into their alcoholic stupor, realize there are no clean plates in the house, so they simply scrape the remains of last night's dinner into the sink and reuse the dirty dishes. During dinner no one is able to chew loudly enough to muffle the sounds of verbal abuse from the irrational, drunk parents who offer (absurdly) stern instructions on table etiquette.

## The Arresting Nature of Grace

I was trapped in this household with no way out, except that once a week I sat before a television and vanished into what seemed to be heaven. Every week an elegantly dressed woman entered a beautifully furnished living room and graciously welcomed me to another evening of *General Electric Theater* (at least it felt like she was speaking directly to me). I never dreamed of missing the program because Loretta Young gave me hope. Although I could not block out the sound of my parents' screaming, I could respond to the beauty I saw despite the ugliness that surrounded me as I sat and watched TV.

God gave me an alternative way of life in Loretta Young. I looked at her beautiful clothes, listened to her gentle voice and watched the respect she showed toward an audience of strangers. It was then that a seed of hope for a different life began to grow in me. I didn't know how to get it, but I was determined that one day I would.

Not long ago, I was walking with a friend in a neighborhood in Ojai, California, when that inkling returned to me as a full-blown reminder of God's faithfulness. We passed a house so incredibly attractive that I was compelled to knock on the door, hoping to congratulate the owner for creating such a beautiful home. My friend stood in amused silence on the sidewalk. The long walkway to the house offered me more than enough time to experience a bit of trepidation. Still, the urge to knock was greater than the urge to flee.

As a woman opened the door, I quickly mustered a *hello*. A bit awkwardly, I slipped into my intended congratulatory statement. Though kind, the stranger was quick to explain that I was talking to the wrong person, as she was simply a guest. The owner, she explained, was throwing a party but surely would welcome my remark. I was instructed to "wait right here."

Moments later, the owner, very pleased with my impression of her house, then turned the tables. She had a surprise of her own: I was invited to tour the inside of her home, and to my shock and utter delight, I learned this house was owned previously by none other than Loretta Young! Memories of this woman's significance surged to my mind. I couldn't help but see that the image Loretta Young projected on television so many years before was a genuine extension of how she lived.

Grace arrests our attention. God will bring it to us, as he did with me, in a way we can best understand. It may first flow into your life by an attractive and pleasing personality like Loretta Young, surrounded by a beautiful home with pleasant landscaping, or it may arrest you through the character of a friend like Lois. Yet those God uses to distribute grace are hardly limited to the beautiful. .

## GRACE IN THE ORDINARY

Graciousness becomes a distinguishing mark of our lives as we experience it for ourselves. Adults who weren't loved as children tend to struggle with the truth that, regardless of what we think, feel or do, God's steadfast love is unconditional. We have to learn to look for his love in the ordinary events of life, just as my friend in Manhattan has.

Over the course of one winter she was twice taken aback by the most unexpected source of grace. She was walking to her office on blustering white days, limping along with the cane that she needed as she recovered from knee surgery. Twice she fell into snow banks. On each occasion she was offered a helping hand from a homeless person. Both times her attention was arrested by the unexpected source of grace and the beauty of kindness she found.

God sends us his grace in just the way we need it. As a child, I needed a different model for how to live. My friend needed not just to be rescued from a snow bank, but to learn to put away prejudices. When Jesus modeled grace for his disciples it literally took their theological breath away. Through both his words and his behavior, he made it clear that all people sin, either by intent or through ignorance—that despite our efforts, we are all spiritually homeless. Our sin creates a barrier between God and us. But he wants us to be in relationship with him and has graciously provided Jesus to bring us home. We can't earn this gift, we don't deserve it, but there it is for us—a free gift, an invitation into God's presence, marked by unconditional, steadfast love.

## A FOREIGN THOUGHT, A NEW LIFE

We learn most about this new grace-filled life through John's account of how Jesus lived. Rather than just relating the important things Jesus said and did, John explains what it all means for us. Near the end of his writing, he reveals his hand:

> Jesus did many other miraculous signs in the presence of his disciples, which are not recorded in this book. But these are written that you may believe that Jesus is the Christ, the Son of God, and that by believing you may have life in his name. (Jn 20:30-31)

John wanted us to make the connection that Jesus is God and that when we receive him into our life, we gain access to his resurrected life, which is boldly marked by the contagious presence of grace. Four times in the last four verses of the prologue to his Gospel (Jn 1:14-18 NRSV), John assigns grace to the character of Jesus.

To understand his whole picture of grace, we need to consider John's immediate audience: they were members of his own crowd, a group of Jews practiced in keeping ideas of grace separated from religious duty. Like many in theocratic cultures, they were accustomed to living scrupulously by religious law in order to be acceptable to God. Their religious teachers vigorously kept the law before them. Knowing this, you can imagine how foreign the notion of grace must have appeared. In fact, the book of Acts, which records the history of the early church, shows that it took years before Christians really understood it. Then, having finally "gotten it" in the first century, the church began to pull away from grace during the second century, establishing a new ecclesiastical law. In human hands such is the fate of so beautiful a thing as grace.

Tragically, even now legalism and judgment are benchmarks of how most nonbelievers view Christianity. Almost without exception when I ask people to explain to me what a Christian is, their response is a variation on this: "A Christian," they say, "is a person who tries to do good things, has to keep a lot of rules and goes to church." This definition often comes with a heavy sigh, which suggests Christianity is mostly about following rules, not living under grace. What I find most fascinating is that a similar perception is held by most Christians as well. It seems that we, too, have a difficult time believing that God's favor is not earned. According to John, the grace of Jesus is needed by all, is available to all and is beneficial to all. "From his fullness we have all received, grace upon grace" (Jn 1:16 NRSV). No wonder it's called *amazing* grace! Amazing, too, is that those who don't yet know him perceive Christians as legalistic and—more amazing still—that Christians often seem to agree!

I am convinced that believers who are effective in witnessing have most likely been arrested by grace. Not only do they understand it theologically, they have experienced it firsthand. In gratitude to God, they are eager to extend this same grace to others. Usually amidst some crisis, Christ's gracious response to their situation came so unexpectedly and brought such undeserved relief that these believers are compelled to share Christ with anyone who is ready to listen. In those moments when the truth of grace captures us, when we surrender our wills as vessels for God's use, we are moved to share with others.

When a believer has been steeped in grace, all the members of his or her immediate society detect a refreshing fragrance. The presence of grace can awaken people from the monotony of their lives, whether they sit in an executive suite or drive a street-sweeper. Grace will restore patience to a young mother herding toddlers through the grocery store and hauling countless loads of laundry from the laundry room to the bedrooms and back again. Grace informs the heart as wonderfully as the *Wall Street Journal* informs the most exuberant corporate investor. Grace brings inspiration to the artist and unexpected harmony to the musician. God's grace makes a difference in who we are, where we are and what we do. God's grace is arresting!

## WORDS, ATTITUDES, ACTIONS

Grace is more than the ability to enter a room easily and speak with a soothing voice. In fact, there are as many ways to experience and understand grace as there are situations and people in the world. The key to it all is that God is the one who opens our spiritual eyes to recognize his grace. Nowhere is this more evident than in evangelism.

At its heart evangelism is a simple practice. The description of evangelism that I find most helpful originated with the Archbishops' Committee of 1918[1] (I've adapted it a bit): *To evangelize is to bring people to Jesus Christ through a combination of word, attitude and action done in the power of the Holy Spirit, in order that non-Christian people will put their trust in God through Jesus, accept him as their Savior and serve him as King in the fellowship of his church.* This is a comprehensive goal that, when lived out, becomes a powerful reality.

Few people will come to Jesus through only the words we speak. Yet when we think of evangelism, we think in terms of conveying words—words of truth, a spoken message. In fact, our words lack credibility if they are not accompanied by acts of compassion. And if our words are inconsistent with our actions, we might as well be silent with unbelievers who are proficient at discerning an incongruent witness.

Witnessing and evangelism are greatly enhanced through a basic understanding of psychology: what makes us think, feel and behave as we do. Gerald May, a psychiatrist and spiritual director, says this:

Regardless of the many forms that spiritual searching can take, and regardless of its origins in consciousness, it is highly unlikely that anyone in the modern West will proceed very far without knocking on the door of psychology. It may be through books or counseling or growth groups, or it may be through psychological discussions with friends. It may come before or after one looks into religion. It may take the form of an intellectual interest in the workings of the mind, or it may be a frantic attempt to create some new kind of experience. But sooner or later, nearly everyone appears at the behavioral sciences' doorstep.[2]

I say, beat these seekers to the door! Gather information about how and why people behave as they do. This is the human side of evangelism; its importance cannot be overstated. I'm not suggesting we become amateur psychologists. I am, however, convinced that we need to broaden our understanding of people.

Part of this process is learning how to be objective about your own life. Perhaps you aren't thinking, feeling or behaving like a gracious Christian just now. What sort of effect is that having on your ability to witness or evangelize? Look at your life and answer these questions: Where does my understanding of the gospel exclude grace? How does my attitude reflect legalism or judgment rather than grace? How might my actions, especially toward those who are helpless or undeserving, reflect grace?

Evangelism has a human dimension and a divine dimension. As evangelists, we become partners with God in the spiritual conversions of those whom he's placed in our sphere of influence. God places in us a concern for the spiritual well-being of our unbelieving friends. Meanwhile, he is creating a spiritual hunger in that person. That's how it happened between Lois and me.

## DRAWN TO GOD

When I remember my relationship with Lois in my pre-Christian days, one word comes to mind: *different.* It's not as though she was larger than life. We struggled through many of the same things. We both made mistakes. But her responses differed because of the presence of the Holy Spirit in her life. Think about it: all of us reach a point when we need a better-than-human solution for a need at hand. When I reached that point, when despair led me to contemplate suicide, God brought Lois to show me a different way.

That difference was the power of God's gracious spirit.

I think Fyodor Dostoyevsky was onto something big when he said, "Beauty will save the world."[3] It makes sense that because I craved the presence of beauty, God used a beautiful person to bring me home. Lois was able to bring me to Jesus because I liked her and I was able to trust her, even to the point of going to her church.

On the day God saved me, my husband and I were taking Lois's children to meet her at church. They had stayed at our home over the weekend, and Lois had volunteered to come get them for church on Sunday. This would have meant about fifty miles of driving for her, since she and her husband, Larry, were spending the weekend out of town. I assured her that it would be no problem for us to take the children to church.

I lied. At that time, Sundays at our house meant relaxing, reading the *Los Angeles Times* and going to the beach. This decision interrupted our routine. Why did I offer? Because I loved Lois and I wanted to help her.

Don and I arranged to meet Lois and Larry at the front door. Everyone was carrying a Bible—except us. There was a guest speaker preaching about the command to honor your father and mother, an immediate problem for me. I was a Yankee liberal, and the preacher was an extremely conservative southerner. Even today, I try to imagine his horror had he known I had recently written a letter to a communist professor at UCLA, pledging my whole-hearted support. The taste of glue from the envelope was still on my lips. How do you think I reacted to this preacher?

Well, by the grace of God, when he talked about honoring your father and mother, the painful message came in loud and clear. I left with a nagging concern: I couldn't honor my mother and father because their behavior as parents was not honorable. I understood the ideal, but I also knew this was impossible. At that moment I wanted to be a Christian but figured I couldn't because I couldn't honor this command.

Little did I know that I was under the conviction of sin. I was stunned. I'd never heard anything about this commandment. I was shocked to see myself as a sinner. Yet even as I felt convicted, I wanted so much to have what I knew Lois had. I felt like a little girl, face pressed against the window of a pet store, longing for a puppy I knew I didn't have the money to buy.

After church my mood was somber. Lois tuned in to what was going on. She was tender without prying. She said she would call me later that afternoon. When she called to ask me how I was, I blurted out that I would like to be a Christian, that I would like to have the kind of life that she had, but that I couldn't because I knew I couldn't follow the command I heard in church that day.

Out of her mouth came the most gentle, gracious words I'd ever heard. "Of course you can't honor them, Chris. God doesn't expect you to. They have been too mean to deserve your honor. But if you ask God, he will give you the Holy Spirit, and he will empower you to do something you cannot humanly do."

"How do I get the Holy Spirit?" I questioned.

"You just ask him to come into your life," she encouraged.

I ended my conversation with Lois, explaining I had something important to do. I hung up, walked across the bright blue carpet in my living room, stared up at the beam ceilings and simply said, "Holy Spirit, come into my life." I didn't confess any sin. I didn't thank Jesus for dying on the cross for me. Nevertheless, peace filled my heart with such quiet power that I knew, without any doubt, that the Holy Spirit had come in. Up to that point, anxiety had ruled my life. Now there was something new, something that I didn't fully understand but that I could not deny.

After receiving Jesus, for the first time in my life I was able to sit down and finish my dinner. I was finally free from the perpetual anxiety stemming from my childhood that prevented me from ever completing a meal.

## THE STORY DOESN'T END THERE!

Thankfully, Lois understood that her commitment to me was not complete on the day I asked God to save me. Those newly born in him will not be sustained in their faith if we do not teach them to *serve Jesus as King in the fellowship of his church.* Lois did this first by her own gracious example. I figured that I was supposed to live as she lived. Immediately, without having heard that I was supposed to do so, I told Don that I was now a Christian. "Don't ask me to explain this because I don't understand it!" I sharply cautioned.

The next morning I called the pastor of the church to set up an appointment. I wanted to tell him and get all the encouragement I could. Nobody told me this was a good thing to do. I just felt the need to get all the help I could. For one thing, my mind was transformed. Suddenly I thought about God all the time. I experienced a stark hunger to read the Bible. I wanted to know how to go about it, and I figured that because the pastor was a "professional" Christian, he was probably the best person to go for this kind of help.

Lois stayed with me through all this. Now our long, frequent conversations were about spiritual things. She never laughed at my questions but took each one seriously and responded with a sense of humor and reason. We began attending a Bible study in Santa Barbara, California. On the forty-five minute drive there and back we talked about the lesson. Lois gently encouraged me in every step I took toward serving Jesus as King. I was baptized in the fall, and Don and I started attending church.

One day during that first year, I picked up my oldest son, Brian, at preschool and his teacher pointed out to me a harmful attitude that was influencing how I disciplined him. I was devastated. As soon as I could, I flew to Lois and explained what had happened. She was merciful. She was kind. And she was graciously firm. She read John 15 slowly to me, explaining each major point. She explained that God prunes our lives through these events so that we can become more like Jesus. She added that we cannot grow without such pruning. She asked if I was willing to pray with her about this. I can still hear her tender voice beckoning me. Pruning wasn't an issue for me once I understood why it was necessary.

In subsequent years Lois and I have talked about this amazing first year of my Christian life. I was so hungry for God, so intent on getting everything he desired for me. We have marveled at how compliant I was, given my strong, independent nature. Again the human and divine elements were working. God was surely motivating me. The Holy Spirit's presence was making profound changes in me. And because I had also lived under the influence of arrogant and rebellious parents, I knew I didn't want to veer off God's path for my life. How Lois lived and how she evangelized me helped me to see the human elements of serving Christ as King. Unfortunately not all of us are as "thoroughly" evangelized: that is, we hear the gospel but we don't see a life transformed by the gospel. But once we grasp how comprehensive the task of evangelism is, we can know what unbelievers need to experience from us in their journey to Christ.

God's grace is available to everyone, everywhere. In *Amazing Grace*, Kathleen Norris describes her experience of it like this:

> One morning this past spring I noticed a young couple with an infant at an airport departure gate. The baby was staring intently at other people, and as soon as he recognized a human face, no matter whose it was, no matter if it was young or old, pretty or ugly, bored or happy or worried-looking he would respond with absolute delight.
>
> It was beautiful to see. Our drab departure gate had become the gate of heaven. And as I watched that baby play with any adult who would allow it, I felt . . . awestruck . . . because I realized that this is how God looks at us, staring into our faces in order to be delighted, to see the creature he made and called good, along with the rest of creation. And, as Psalm 139 puts it, darkness is as nothing to God, who can look right through whatever evil we've done in our lives to the creature made in the divine image.[4]

Oh, for eyes to see like that baby's! Oh, for a heart to love like God's! Grace is so wonderful a word, so great a gift. Isn't it time we give it a greater space in our attitude toward those who are open to God?

---

## ENGAGE IN BECOMING GRACIOUS

---

1. What strikes you as important in this chapter? Explain why.

2. Read John 7:53—8:11 aloud slowly. Imagine that you are the woman in the story. (You may need to read this Scripture more than once to get the "feel" of her experience.)

   a. How are you feeling as you stand before this crowd?

   b. How does Jesus treat you graciously?

   c. What difference does this make in how you feel about Jesus? How you feel about yourself?

   d. What are you motivated to do after this encounter?

3. What kind of *human* response might you have toward an unbeliever caught in sin?

4. How does this story convey to you what a *divine* response to sin actually looks like?

5. In the last chapter, you made a list of people you would like to influence for Christ. Pray for each person on your list. Ask God what you could do to demonstrate his grace to them.

Prayerfully and intentionally strive to complete these actions. Write down your feelings and the response of your unbelieving friends as you follow through. Sharing the ups and downs of your experiences with other believers will be helpful to you and to them!

# 3

# FOCUSED

## WITNESSING AS YOUR VOCATION

*[Vocation is] the place where your deep gladness
and the world's deep hunger meet.*

FREDERICK BUECHNER

*Meanwhile his disciples urged him,
"Rabbi, eat something."
But he said to them,
"I have food to eat that you know nothing about."
Then his disciples said to each other,
"Could someone have brought him food?"
"My food," said Jesus, "is to do the will of him who sent me
and to finish his work."*

JOHN 4:31-34

**TO BE FOCUSED** on something simply means
that we concentrate on it. Evangelism depends on focus, and the task of evangelism becomes much easier
when we develop a credo based on our unique personality, natural talents and spiritual gifts.

My friend Stan is terrified of evangelism. He's a new Christian from a thoroughly secular background, and while he appreciates the beauty of evangelism done well, he shudders at the idea of being involved in it himself.

Oh, but witness he does. Without realizing it he has quite willingly taken the first small steps of evangelism. Recently he underwent surgery for a melanoma, which was removed with no signs of cancer beyond the primary site. Stan fully understood his life-threatening situation and was convinced by the resulting lab report that God had intervened for him. Nobody had to encourage him to tell others; he simply and openly spoke of his experience to his friends: "God answers prayer. He has saved my life."

Stan is what Garrison Keillor sometimes calls a "shy Christian." He probably wouldn't be described as being naturally bold, but he, like most of us, talks easily about the things that are important to him. And as he comes to a deeper understanding of God's importance in his life, it is natural for him to talk about Jesus with others.

For many of us the problem with evangelism lies in learning how to link our spiritual experiences with our general experiences so we can convey them easily to our unbelieving friends. This is the step at which we struggle with our own fear of speaking up and with the fear of others' negative reaction. Actually, witnessing is a natural response to any good news. It's what people do when they gush over the merits of cable versus DSL, rave over a particular movie or wholeheartedly support a football team.

We need to remember that *evangelism* is not a synonym for *witness;* this is what frees Stan on the one hand and frightens him on the other. Every Christian, regardless of where she or he is along the path of growth, is a witness in one way or another. Evangelism, however, depends on the use of gifts and skills that often come later in our spiritual development. Not every Christian will be an evangelist, but

many (more than we think) can be trained in evangelism. As we focus on our vocational credo by living in light of it, God will present
to us many more opportunities for evangelism. We will be competent
in whatever evangelistic situation God brings to us if we choose to
develop the skills introduced in this book.

## OUR DEEPEST NEED: MEANING

One of these skills is recognizing our meaningful experiences. I
learned about this while cleaning toilets. I was an intense twenty-
five-year-old longing to build a meaningful life. I knew being a good
wife and mother was a valuable endeavor, so I had resolved to ded-
icate myself to that end. As you might imagine, doubts of so lofty a
domestic goal crept in—especially since *domestic* was a fairly unat-
tractive word to me! Often I battled the suspicion that meaningful
life only occurred outside our home. In my pre-motherhood days
love of the arts, social causes and international events had given my
life meaning. In my most honest moments I now resented my two
preschool-age sons, believing they were distractions from my search
for significance.

One particular Friday I was at home cleaning. I didn't (and still
don't) like housework, so it was not an exciting day. I was a new Christian, deeply involved in a challenging study of the apostle Paul's life,
and I longed for more time to investigate this rich material. Instead, in
a very ordinary moment, I found myself cleaning toilets and simulta-
neously refereeing my sons, who were vying over who owned which
toy. In that very moment of cleaning and corralling, a thought crashed
into my mind. *Since I am doing what I believe God wants me to do at this
point in my life, then how I do what God wants me to do is as important as
what I do.* Suddenly significance shone through the tedium.

Yes, I knew that my salvation meant that I was going to heaven
one day. But I hadn't understood what Paul meant when he said in
Romans 5:10: "Having been reconciled, we will be saved by his life."
At that moment I realized that "being saved by his life" could take
place wherever I was, in all that I did, as long as I consented to letting

the life of Jesus influence how I handled the moment.

God has designed for our salvation, his perfect gift to us, to become increasingly real, applicable and valuable to us over time. We want our non-Christian friends to know and to experience all that we have come to understand through our relationship with God. As we realize how God uses our lives, new meaning covers each day. With this new meaning comes an enthusiasm for sharing what we're experiencing in Christ.

Oliver Wendell Holmes, who understood that the meaning of life can be elusive, warned, "Most people go to their graves with their music still inside them."[1] Missed meaning happens for two reasons: we haven't identified the song to be sung, or we let other things get in the way of ever learning our tune. It's my belief that for Christians, singing our song must involve understanding our vocation and using the opportunities it brings to be channels for witnessing.

If witnessing is the melody, vocation is the staff on which the notes rest. For example, when I meet young mothers struggling with tedium, I can identify with their human need for significance. If I am kind and courteous to them, a door often opens through which I can sing, figuratively speaking. Literally, speaking is the key. I identify with their struggle, I earn the right to be heard, and then I talk about how, with God's help, I tackled this issue.

## CREATED FOR HIS PURPOSES

Ordinarily we think of vocation in connection to our daily work, our occupation as homemaker, executive, firefighter, clerk or whatever demands we set the alarm clock at night and moan at its authority in the early morning. That's our job. However, the root of the word *vocation* has to do with being called. For our purpose, *vocation* is the purpose God has for us as "new creatures" in Jesus Christ.

Certainly vocation is an important concept for Christians to apply to any job. It lifts our daily occupation from a matter of economic survival to a part of what God has sovereignly created us to be and do in Jesus Christ.

Imagine that your phone is ringing. Your beloved father is thinking of you and dials your number, hoping you will pick up and engage in conversation with him. He longs to speak to you. He wants you to listen to what he has to say. He knows it won't be easy for you to say yes, but he's inviting you on a trip, all expenses paid. He's calling to discuss the details. To be honest, this offer sounds wonderful; but realistically, because of your full schedule, your workload and your commitments, you see this trip as a nice but remote possibility. On the phone you sigh and beg pardon: "I cannot come. . . . I have crops and commitments. I've got a cow to milk, a woman to marry and bills to pay. And I'm coaching a Little League team." Got the picture? It's no wonder, then, that when the phone rings, we already resent being interrupted.

In Scripture we discover that our heavenly Father places a calling—a vocation—on each of us. He's mapped out a route for your life, along which you will meet unbelievers prepared for unique witness. It's a trip that takes a lifetime; and it will take eternity to sort out all God did through your witness. Your route may seem inconvenient at first, but once you're in heaven you will meet people who are there because someone you witnessed to witnessed to them. They came to know Jesus, one by one. And they brought members of their families and some of their friends.

Our destinations are custom designed. When the Father knit us together in our mother's womb (Ps 139:13), he stitched in all the specific resources each of us needs for this journey. He created us for the purpose of representing himself to the people he places in our lives. Thankfully, he has provided all we need for this trip. We have natural talents and spiritual gifts designed to guide others to Jesus, the one who can meet their needs. Though our destinations are delightfully varied, one thing remains certain: each of us is called and equipped to share his good news through our attitudes, actions and words.

As Jesus told his followers, "All authority in heaven and on earth has been given to me. Therefore go and make disciples of all nations" (Mt 28:18-19), and "You will receive power when the Holy Spirit comes on you; and you will be my witnesses in Jerusalem, and in all Judea and Samaria, and to the ends of the earth" (Acts 1:8, the last words Jesus spoke to his disciples).

If the situation were not so serious, our ignoring these commands would seem as comical as toddlers ignoring their parents' call. Clearly God calls each of us to share his message. His Son commands it and his Holy Spirit gives us the ability to do it. Lest we forget, something amazing is found in obedience to this call.

## WITNESSING AND YOUR NATURAL TALENTS

All this talk of vocation may tempt us to reason that the responsibility for witnessing belongs only to evangelists (that rare breed we appreciate but are relieved not to be one of), but Scripture tells us that God calls each of us to witness: "Anyone who believes in the Son of God has this testimony in his heart. . . . And this is the testimony: God has given us eternal life, and this life is in his Son" (1 Jn 5:10-11).

Further, God's call to us is personal. God calls each of us to witness in a unique way. (Take a deep breath.) We are not called to absorb the style of successful evangelists. My work and yours is simply to assess how God is leading us.

Richard Leider and David Shapiro have written a marvelous book on vocation entitled *Whistle While You Work*. The following excerpt from their book includes my evangelistic content in brackets.

> There are as many callings in the world [to witness] as there are people [Christians] on the planet. This isn't to say that other people might not do the same things we do or that they can't be passionate about the identical issues that compel us. It does, however, mean that each of us is called directly; no one else is called to do the same things we are *in the same manner we are*. Our calling [to witness, and even to evangelize] is our embedded destiny; it is the seed of our identity. . . . *Heeding* our calling involves a conscious choice to be ourselves—to uncover in the here and now our God-given nature.[2]

God intends for us to be ourselves. He gives us a unique disposition and a unique set of abilities. He gives us natural talents at our natural birth. Spiritual gifts, as described in the New Testament, are given by God at the time of our spiritual rebirth. Our responsibility is to be obedient in response to our calling, in accordance with our personality and using his gifts in the circumstances he provides us. That we get to be involved in something so important should cause our minds to reel!

## GETTING FOCUSED

Our vocation is to witness, and our natural gifts enhance this eternal assignment. Having understood that, we must now focus on that calling.

Typically when I envision a focused person, I picture someone with a furrowed brow and a face drawn in deep thought. Recently I encountered a young father who challenged this stereotype. We were in San Diego for Thanksgiving weekend, having Sunday breakfast in a crowded restaurant. Patrons throughout were engaged in lively conversation. Waitresses whirled by, accommodating the needs of the animated and hungry crowd. And there, in the center of the chaos, sat a new father, oblivious to all but his infant son. He held the baby in one arm while stroking the newborn's soft skin with his free hand. He radiated delight. He was laughing, talking to this new arrival as though the child could understand every word. The scene was extraordinary, really. I can't ever recall witnessing a father (or mother, for that matter) so focused on a baby for forty-five minutes in a public place.

In that restaurant it occurred to me that this is how God treats each one of his children. This is how he wants us to act toward each other: focused but not rigid, present but not smothering, absorbed in reciprocal communication amidst chaos, thoroughly enjoying one another, doing what we can to help when problems arise.

*Focus* is a word used both as a noun and a verb; each use is necessary to our quest. A point of focus (noun) is essential to clarity. We have to know what is being closely examined. When a sailor examines a chart, he or she spends little time giving it a general overview. A specific starting point, route and destination are what matters. A point of focus is particular.

When we focus (verb) our attention on a subject, we *concentrate*. Donald Laird provides us with a vivid description of this: "We must work at the right things and in the right direction, keep on the main road and off the detours."[3] Nowhere is it more necessary that we focus our attention than in fulfilling our Christian calling. Nowhere is there a greater chance for distraction or inhibition to keep us from the countless opportunities God brings our way. We must keep our eyes on Christ. The Gospels are full of stories of how he focused on individuals.

## FOCUS ON CHRIST

Jesus sat down by a well in Samaria (Jn 4:4-42), exhausted from the day's trip. The sun's rays were beating down. This journey with his disciples to Samaria had begun shortly after dawn. For hours Christ walked over rock-strewn hills. Surely the terrain itself proved taxing, demanding they be attentive to the threat of bandits.

Imagine walking with him that day and sighting the well! After quenching your thirst, you'd probably want to relieve your tired feet in the shade. But in this account we see that Christ did something totally different, something that required astute focus on his part.

Jesus noticed a woman approaching the well. Because he is who he is, he knew that she had been married five times, was now living with a man and was apparently shunned by her disapproving neighbors. We can glean these insights from the details that John provides in his Gospel. In ancient Israel the well was the gathering place for women— a place to chat and keep up with the latest news. Almost always the women would arrive early in the morning to avoid the stifling heat of midday. So the Samaritan woman's timing is the first clue to her needs. She comes to the well under the suffocating noonday sun. Evidently her intention was to avoid the other women, for why else would she break tradition or endure the conditions at hand? And it is here that we see a focused Jesus seizing an opportunity that requires that he move beyond his own circumstances and desires.

For starters, he breaks with all Jewish tradition by approaching a woman, and to double the offense, a Samaritan woman. John tells us that Jews had no dealings with Samaritans. Certainly this woman was not expecting to enter into a conversation. Yet Jesus initiated one by enlisting her help. He needed a drink, which was something she could offer. The water she offered provided Christ with an illustration of the living water of the Holy Spirit. She was taken aback by his acknowledgment of her five failed marriages and her present fruitless relationship.

But that's not the end of the story. With ease Jesus shifted the conversation to a subject of greater hope—that of living water and good news of his messiahship, the very event she and her people awaited. Along with other disciples, John witnessed this surprising exchange and its results. The woman leaves her water pot, runs to the city and, despite being discounted for her moral laxity, boldly talks with joy about her encounter with Jesus.

"Many of the Samaritans from that town believed in him because of the woman's testimony, 'He told me everything I ever did' " (Jn 4:39). What a powerful story! What an incredible display by the Messiah himself, of how focused vocation reaped a precious harvest for the kingdom of God, of how gently he offered hope to one who seemed terribly close to despair.

## AMY'S STORY

Amy is a woman focused on her vocation and capable of easy transitions between witnessing and evangelism. We have served in ministry together in many capacities over the years. Her vocation shines through every thing I've ever seen her do. "My vocation," says Amy, "is to love people and move them one step closer to God." This resolve remains intact whether she's interacting with those who don't know Christ or working in a Christian context. Her strongest natural gifts are enthusiasm, flexibility and creativity. She identifies her spiritual gifts as exhortation, helps, teaching and pastoral roles. It's notable that she doesn't see evangelism as one of her gifts.

A few years ago Amy had to seek out a salaried position to pay college expenses for her two children. Her initial job search proved quite discouraging. Every avenue she pursued presented insurmountable roadblocks. This was surprising, since Amy is an articulate woman who exudes confidence. During this season she spent a weekend away with her girlfriends. As she listened to each of them relay stories of their interesting work, her heart took a turn. She realized that finding a job was not something she could attain through her own efforts. It was at that moment, in the middle of it all, that she excused herself and left the room. Settled in a private place, she dropped to her knees and pleaded with the Lord to lead her to a job that would meet her needs and fulfill his purpose in her.

The next Monday morning a man she had once worked with called. Their paths hadn't crossed for nearly twenty-five years. Her name came to mind, he said, as someone who might know some hard-working woman that needed a job. He was seeking an office employee to fill a position like the one Amy once held.

Amazed by God's timely provision, but still lacking total assurance that this was the job for her, Amy opted to visit the office prior to accepting the position. She met each person and afterwards felt peace about taking the job. The office was located in a vast business complex, but she would have daily contact with only four other employees. On the first day of work Amy started genuinely listening to her coworkers. She established one rule for herself: "I get paid to do my job, I do not get paid to witness." Creative as she was, she knew she would have to earn the right to speak into her coworkers lives.

So Amy arrived at work early, stayed late and set dates with coworkers for lunch, coffee breaks or conversation after work. She'd listen and ask questions, searching each encounter for an appropriate response. Before long Amy understood the issues of each of her coworkers. With these discoveries it became apparent that none of them enjoyed a support system.

Amy's efforts required a great deal of focus. We all know that meaningful relationships take time. Amy kept on, watchful for opportunities. "If people don't open up on their own," she explained, "I pay attention to what excites or motivates them." In such instances, Amy would ask herself, "What is this particular person's passion? What is of particular interest to them?" Before ever using words, Amy watched for clues leading her to meaningful contact. What did she find? Her colleagues had many concerns: death, divorce, separation, abandonment, finances, work issues and parenting problems. Later, she observed how holidays affected her new friends, how cultural or current events impacted them and how they handled ups and downs in the company.

Taking these clues into prayerful consideration, Amy took the next step, which by this time was natural and nonthreatening. "I'd ask a person a question about a concern or an interest I'd identified. When there was a pause in conversation, I'd return to the subject and ask an open question, one that couldn't be answered with a *yes* or *no*." From there Amy made a pledge to God. She knew that he'd given that job to her. She wanted to be faithful to this assignment. So she promised to do everything she could to bring each of her colleagues to Christ. She would find ways to encourage each one and go through the doors that God opened. Not surprisingly, doors swung easily on the hinge of generosity. Amy used personal but inexpensive gifts as a means of saying that others were important to her, that they were in her thoughts even when she was not in their company.

It's important to state that none of Amy's behavior was contrived. It flowed naturally from her inner life with God. She loved these people, and it was natural for her to give them gifts. Still, even here she considered their needs. She resolved to give in a way that the recipient never felt indebted. Because she focused on each person and gave meaningful gifts, the receiver was left only to conclude that this was a natural expression of Amy's listening.

One coworker was a woman I'll call Linda. She had a blended family of four children. Understandably, Linda faced incredible challenges in juggling all her responsibilities. She was often exhausted.

Amy encouraged her in every way that her own busy schedule allowed. On Halloween, Christmas and Valentine's Day she brought cards or little gifts for each of the four children. She didn't talk about God until the door was opened for her. That opportunity came when Linda told her about her father's death. As it turns out, Linda was a Christian but she had not gone to church for many years, nor had she done anything to nurture her relationship with God. She was living in a spiritual desert and Amy provided an oasis. Before long, Linda began talking to God again.

Tracy was a young coworker who had been caught up in a promiscuous life. She desperately wanted to settle down and get married, so when she met a man twenty years her senior, she married him, hoping this was the fulfillment of her dream. Her husband was financially successful, but shortly after the marriage it was discovered that he had terminal cancer. Amy walked with Tracy through his death and comforted her as she experienced deep sadness and loss. Amy baked her bread, brought her tea bags and prayed with her and for her. Eventually, the two women had a conversation where Tracy disclosed to Amy that she needed God, and she started going to church and soon became a Christian.

Dan was an older man in the office who was carrying a burden of grief because his wife had left him. He was depressed and vulnerable, but he was also very witty. It didn't take Amy long to see that he responded best to jokes and to questions about his cat. She began collecting jokes for Dan. She brought treats for his cat. At Christmas she gave him a book her church had published with stories of how different people connected with God. When he finished reading it, he began reading it again. Soon he told Amy about the years he attended church in his youth. He realized how important spirituality was to him and how far from God he was. Eventually he, too, rededicated his life to Jesus and began attending church.

Amy spoke with tenderness as she told me about her last coworker, Fay, "a dear, dear, humble woman" who was married to a man who carelessly spent nearly everything they had and drank nearly anything he could find. He lived for these vices and for keeping up appearances. Time after time Fay returned from an exhausting workday to face the pressure to ignore home duties and join him for a night of clubs and partying. He wanted a sexy drinking buddy. She wanted a husband who loved her and was interested in their children, children who were drifting toward addictions of their own.

Fay enjoyed little things, so Amy would occasionally pick up a knickknack or catalog (another of Fay's favorite things) and drop it by her desk. They talked frequently about her marriage, and Amy remained focused on the larger picture, never being critical or giving advice. Each time a crisis occurred in Fay's family, Amy would tell her that God was the one person who would never let her down. One day Fay prayed with Amy to receive Christ and her salvation immediately became real.

Amy's natural gifts include being creative and artistic. You can see that in the creative ways she demonstrated love to her coworkers. Often creative people lack focus because they are so apt to be attracted to a variety of interesting things. Yet as soon as Amy realized the issues these good people wrestled with, she understood that God had placed her in that job to influence them for his kingdom.

When Amy describes her two years in this office, she says she simply "barreled in," jumping in wherever something was going on. "This was not a casual commitment," she reminded me. "I kept my focus by praying for each of them at least once daily. I made a pledge to God to rejoice with those who rejoiced in the office and weep with those who wept there."

Amy focused her life within the boundaries of her vocational credo: "I live to love people and bring them one step closer to God." Everything she did flowed from God's life within her.

## NO WIGGLE ROOM

You and I have different natural or spiritual gifts. We weren't sent to *that* office. Each of us is placed where God wants us to be. He gives us all we need to evangelize the people who are among us. Really it comes down to this: once we understand and believe that God has called us to be his witnesses where we are, and once we stand assured that he has given us the authority and power adequate to that task, we can focus on living out our vocation with the people he brings our way.

Lastly, like it or not, there is no wiggle room when it comes to witnessing. Scripture clearly calls all Christians to witness. Only it's a positive expectation, like expecting that our friend would gladly tell us about a wonderful surprise birthday party his buddies planned. It's *good news* we talk about. The vitality of experiencing God in our various vocations is the key.

Evangelism is like witnessing in that it proclaims good news, but it goes a step further. Evangelism is *witnessing with the intention to aid in the reconciliation of a particular person with God.* The New Testament does not seem to expect all Christians to be evangelists. Nevertheless, evangelism is something all Christians are invited to try; and often in the trying, we discover it is a gift we were given. There will probably come a time when, like Amy, we are placed in a situation where what is important to us (that which we can summarize in a credo) becomes part of how God leads us into full-blown evangelism. In this way, evangelism is not nearly so frightening, for the first steps have been small and appealing.

## ENGAGE IN BECOMING FOCUSED

Because the exercises below are so important, they will take more time to complete than the exercises in other chapters. You may decide to develop your vocational credo (question 5) at another time, but aim to do so sometime before the end of this study.

1. What insights in this chapter did you find important?

2. How do you feel about witnessing as *your* vocation? (See Mt 28:18-20; Acts 1:8.)

3. You can discover what avenues God might use to draw you into witnessing and evangelism by answering the following questions: What fills your heart with song? What makes you feel truly alive? What gives you joy? What are you enthusiastic about? The answers to these questions will give you clues about how and where you will be used by God. For example, are you drawn to creating things, to writing rather than talking, to enjoying nature? Do you prefer a crowded city, interacting with others, performing before an audience, being at a party? Do you enjoy having a one-on-one conversation, going shopping, visiting an art gallery, playing tennis, dining at a fine restaurant where the food and service is meticulous? Or do you like relaxing at a hamburger joint or playing games in a video arcade? Do you like working with your hands, operating things, researching information, making deals, or solving problems? Do you like routine or change? Are you someone who loves solitude or are you energized by crowds? What gives you a personal sense of accomplishment—doing something or being something? Are you motivated by material rewards or an inner sense of accomplishment? Are you an encourager? Do you see the big picture or are you a detail person?

4. After you have considered these questions, take a piece of paper and do the following exercise.

   a. Write down five things that *come easily* to you (e.g., gardening, grooming dogs, critiquing a play, teaching songs to children, shopping, working on machinery, organizing things or tearing things apart).

   b. Write down five things that *energize* you—the things that make you get up and go even when you are tired.

   c. Now write down any complimentary labels that have been given to you (e.g., peacemaker, leader, life of the party, great with animals, dependable, good in a crisis, mechanical whiz).

   Look over your answers. Ask your friends and family for their input. You might be surprised at the responses you get. Use your lists and any input you receive from others as springboards for developing a full picture of your talents, gifts and interests. See how God has uniquely created you. Notice how he has already provided you with an arena for the use of your gifts and talents.

As I have considered these questions, I find what comes most naturally for me is interacting with people and exploring the intangibles of life. I get a kick out of designing Bible studies and creating written content based on research. I relish the opportunity to encourage people who are embarking on anything enterprising. I can guarantee you that my personal avenues for evangelism don't naturally lie in areas of working with my hands, numerical figures or physical things. This doesn't mean that I can't relate to people who have gifts and natural talents in those areas, only that I must find ways to relate other than a shared nature.

When you begin to recognize your natural gifts, you will logically identify some of the destinations on your witnessing journey. It should be noted that God does not simply put people into your life who have natural gifts similar to your own. Nevertheless, we should not be surprised that God uses us in areas that we are naturally comfortable in.

5. Using the insights you have gained from the above questions, you are now ready to develop a vocational credo, a short phrase you can easily memorize that describes what you believe to be your purpose in life. Your credo needs to contain an active verb. Here are some examples:

- I exist to *create* beauty in things and in people.

- I exist to *discover* the God-place in people and help them develop it.

- I exist to *encourage* others to be the best people they can be.

- I exist to *teach* people how to live peaceably together.

If you're like me, developing a vocational credo will take more time than you expect and will probably require several attempts. Suppose your credo is "I exist to encourage others to be the best they can be." This means that when you're standing in the express line beneath a large sign that reads "Limited to Ten Items or Fewer" and the man in front of you has thirteen items in his cart, you pull up your credo and ask God, right then and there, to give you an idea about whether or how to encourage this man. Maybe you will become aware of how you might pray for him. It also means that when a coworker looks discouraged, you find ways to encourage her. No matter what you look for—ways or words—reflect on how God would graciously respond in these situations.

Ultimately I came up with this as my vocational credo: I exist to express the fullness of God's being in every area of my life. Now, since I'm a writer and educator, that credo works for me. Expressing the fullness of God's being is simply a pleasant way for me to say "glorifying God." This means that I use my mind, my emotions, my actions and my natural and spiritual gifts as a means of expression. I notice sunsets and will talk to strangers who are observing the same sunset. Often such incidents lead to significant conversations. It means that I praise people when I see them do something positive in God's world. It involves complimenting people who are trying hard. It seems to me that my credo has as many applications as there are characteristics that show the fullness of God's being.

Once you've developed your credo, apply it to your participation in the world around you. In your office, at home, while you're out and about, *focus* on it. Write it on Post-It notes and put it on your computer in the office, your bathroom mirror or the dashboard of your car. Above all, give yourself room to make mistakes and occasionally even fail. I am terribly aware that a vocational credo does not instantly or ever become a faultless habit.

# 4
# PURE IN HEART

## SOLITARY REFINEMENT

*If there is joy in the world, surely the man of pure heart possesses it.*

THOMAS À KEMPIS


*Blessed are the pure in heart,*

*for they will see God.*

MATTHEW 5:8


**TO BE PURE** in heart means to live with a single-minded purpose of living for the praise of God rather than for the praise of fellow human beings. In evangelism, God uses the pure of heart to clean out wounds in others resulting from sin.

A couple of years ago I was teaching in Buenos Aires along with another professor, Matt. From the moment of our arrivals, each of us was frequently told not to miss visiting a tango bar, where the national dance of Argentina was expertly performed. For one good reason after another this visit was put off till our last night in town.

Nothing really comes alive in South America until after midnight, but, mercifully, our host secured tickets for an early "tourist performance," at 11:00 p.m. at the city's oldest tango bar. Exhausted from the challenge of teaching intensive graduate courses, and stifling our yawns, we set out for this adventure. We were not alone. A German couple also braved the hour, accompanied by their two children, a girl about five and a boy about seven. Noticing their arrival, I figured we would be treated not only to the dancing, but also to the accompaniment of whining youngsters.

Finally, at 11:30, the performance began for an audience of about eight. If so small a group of onlookers discouraged the performers, no one would have known it. Apparently, nothing dampens the heart and soul of tango. The drama, the precision, the costumes and the music were simply out of this world. The pride these Argentinians felt, offering their world-famous tango, electrified the room. I was mesmerized when suddenly Matt poked my arm and pointed to the children. Their eyes were wide open, riveted in wonder. They were much too engrossed to move and far too engaged to whine. Their faces sent this clear message: "We are captured by a truly remarkable sight." I like to think that perhaps after it was all over, one of them tugged on their father's sleeve and said, "Dad, this is the best night of my life!"

## SEEING IS BELIEVING

What does this have to do with purity? After all, the tango isn't known for producing it! Never mind. I'm going after that captivated look on the faces of the children. This is the kind of seeing Jesus promised the pure in heart—eyes opened wide at seeing something remarkable. Jesus claims that when we act from the basis of purity, we will see God doing remarkable things. In the final analysis, if we aren't wide-eyed by the wonder of God, what do we have to share with our unbelieving friends? What will pull them away from unbelief to a life of faith?

The New Testament presents situation after situation where habitually religious people established and maintained meticulous outward acts of purity and yet had hearts that were foul. This hypocrisy deeply troubled Jesus, and here's what he said about it. "It is from within, from the human heart, that evil intentions come: fornication, theft, murder, adultery, avarice, wickedness, deceit, licentiousness, envy, slander, pride, folly. All these evil things come from within and they defile a person" (Mk 7:21-23 NRSV).

Purity is not the result of hiding from reality or somehow escaping the evidence of societal foolishness. In fact, as we deliberately live out our vocational credo, we are bound to rub shoulders with people who practice many of the unsavory acts found on Jesus' list. In this circumstance, we are protected by our intentional development of purity. The pure in heart are those who practice single-mindedness, sincerity and freedom from mixed motives. The pure in heart live for the praise of God and not for the praise of their fellow human beings (see Jn 12:43). But let's face it: in this day and age the word *purity* brings to mind self-righteousness and stern restraint. The word sounds narrow and archaic. But is it? What sort of people do we find in this category?

## BEING PURE IN HEART

Richard Wurmbrand, a Romanian pastor who was imprisoned for his faith before the fall of communism, is someone who could be called "pure in heart." He describes his situation as follows:

> Out of fourteen years in jail under the Communists in Rumania, I
> spent three years alone in a cell thirty feet below ground, never seeing

sun, moon or stars, flowers or snow, never seeing another man except
for the guards and interrogators who beat and tortured me.[1]

During that agonizing time, Wurmbrand grappled with deep issues of faith and won. Here's how he did it. He preached sermons to
God and the invisible angels in his cell. In the hope that he might one
day be released, he memorized these sermons by putting the main
ideas into short rhymes, keeping them in his memory through constant repetition. When, finally, he was set free, he had memorized
about 350 sermons. After his release he went throughout the world
telling about his experiences of "seeing God" in his pitch-black cell.
On the occasion I was privileged to see him speak, his eyes resem-
bled those of the children in the tango bar. Wurmbrand provides us
with a rare example of one pure in heart.

Our lives are quite different from Wurmbrand's, but we too are
tempted to abandon purity. Only unlike the temptations and threats
that arose in a dank solitary cell, our distractions from purity are often innocuously disguised as pleasure. In contrast to Wurmbrand,
we are bombarded by distracting sensations that taunt our single-
mindedness. We are deluged by public messages suggesting the
right to please ourselves or to justify arbitrarily set social standards.
But like Wurmbrand, our task is to focus on the characteristic of purity and to be intentionally captured by its beauty.

## SOLITARY REFINEMENT

Purity—that is, living without deception for the praise of God rather
than for our fellow human beings—is neither small nor easy. To engage in it requires solitary refinement: taking God's perspective into
account as we make moral and behavioral choices. Wurmbrand's
choices to be pure meant both that he went to prison and that in prison
he experienced God. Though our lives are strewn with clutter and
noise, if we are to be focused and pure in heart in fulfilling our call to
evangelize, we must be radically attentive to Jesus.

This is our challenge and our privilege. Each of us is unique. Our experiences and personalities uniquely determine our possibilities of influence. Add to that our talents, style and spiritual gifting, and we realize that no one else is where we are or able to do what we can do. Only, like the tango dancers, we realize there are some basic "steps" that do not vary from dancer to dancer. If we let Jesus capture us as the tango captured those two children, we will be ready to take our joyful place in building God's kingdom.

One day I saw a woman in the gym wearing a T-shirt with this caption: "If you can't run with the big dogs, stay on the porch." The sweat pouring from those of us at the gym that day indicated we were far from the porch. We were all grunting our way through a workout ordeal because we were committed to physical fitness. Purity of commitment belongs to tango dancers and to fitness seekers at the gym. Spiritually speaking, purity is not the property of the proudly pious ones parked on the porch, purse-lipped and naysaying. Purity is the result of sweat and hard spiritual exercise. It is the result of resolve; it is not for the faint of heart.

I suggest that for the purpose of evangelism, being pure in heart means nothing short of letting God's priorities and authoritative rule energize our lives and spirit. In other words, we seek God's way of thinking, feeling and behaving. Through our well-trained thoughts, emotions and behaviors, God's kingdom is brought into and applied to our sphere of influence. Our eyes will open wide in wonder as we see the result. God is the master choreographer, turning evangelism into remarkable rhythm and footwork.

## PURITY AND PAIN

Joy was once defined for me as an experience of God that goes deeper than pain or pleasure. Wurmbrand, for example, thought of his time in prison as the most valuable season in his life because during that time God was so palpably real. Upon leaving the prison he stretched his arms against the outside wall, kissed it and praised God for his experiences there.

The irony here is that great joy nearly always comes after we face

suffering and learn from it. It seems that God has deliberately designed us to come to joy this way. Frederick Buechner writes elo-
quently about our need to become "a good steward of our pain."[2] "It
involves," says Buechner, "taking the risk of being open, of reaching
out, of keeping in touch with the pain as well as the joy of what happens because at no time more than at a painful time do we live out of
the depths of who we are instead of out of the shallows."[3] When we
are living in a place of redemption, the pain we endure pales in com-
parison to the joy we find.

Years before reading Buechner, I discovered this truth. Don and I
had been married about ten years when we acknowledged reoccurring problems, which had begun soon after the wedding. I was talking to my friend and mentor Barbara Pine about these problems, and
she began to ask me some questions. One of them was, "What was
your father like?"

Haltingly I responded, "Mostly he was drunk so I don't know
what he was really like. But I have this reoccurring memory of him
drunk, reeling naked in our living room. He was waving a gun into
the air and saying he was going to kill all of us."

I was thirty years old when I told Barbara that story. I don't think
I had ever shared that memory with anyone before. Powerful feelings of fear tug at me even now as I write about it. Barbara wisely and
gently responded, "You know, Chris, these kinds of experiences
probably have an impact on how you relate now to Don. Maybe time
with a Christian counselor would help you."

Soon after that I walked into a Christian counselor's office without
a clue of what counseling might involve. In very little time his gentle
questions blew the door off my cellar of secrets. I left that office profoundly depressed and afraid because I discovered how much childhood anger and fear still held me captive; and I saw that unless I dealt
with the pain, it was mine for life. Waves of anxiety slapped me senseless. It was as though a huge light had settled on a pile of festering de-
bris. I doubted that I could face what I had kept hidden for so long.

The following morning I got on my knees before God, told him my fears and asked for his help. I wailed in sorrow. When I quieted down, these words came to me: "Unless you walk through this door, Chris, you cannot be my disciple."

Some of my Christian brothers and sisters at the church we were attending did not understand my decision to seek a counselor's help in addressing my dark quagmire. One good friend said kindly, "Chris, it's time to forget what lies behind you." The problem with this advice was that I didn't know how to grasp this shapeless, insidious stuff, let alone "put" it somewhere.

I know the message to open the door to counseling was from God, and I thank him for being clear. Gradually I came to understand that emotional and spiritual growth, though different, are nevertheless intrinsically linked. Consequently, I walked hesitantly and fearfully into the past. For a few years I functioned on nothing but sheer obedience, but through the pain God brought joy. When this process ended, I felt like Wurmbrand—stretching my arms out, touching what had been a prison and carrying away from it a healthy heart and spirit. My counselor gave me this prayer then: "Make us glad for as many days as you have afflicted us, for as many years as we have seen trouble" (Ps 90:15).

I share my story with you because many people today, inside and outside the church, have experiences similar to mine. To be pure in heart in our evangelism does not mean that we must be perfectly free of impurities; but we must be in the process of having our impurities purged. The one who is pure in heart can face and handle her own pain and then, having done that, can face others' pain.

Now I look at the traumatic events I suffered through as a child as my most valuable growth experiences. God has taken the sting away. He has given me knowledge of his faithfulness that I can't imagine having learned any other way. For every deep pain I examined, I cherish an even deeper level of God's comfort. I embrace these events and see value in them. God has brought me relief, but he has also used my past to open doors of opportunity. I am still (though I should not be) often surprised how in pain even the most spiritually belligerent begin to cast about, looking for hope. If we have paid attention to our teacher, Jesus, and if we have learned the steps, God will allow us to demonstrate the dance of redemption for others. I think of evangelism as hope set to a holy tune.

Buechner says, "Life is not for sissies no matter who you are or where or how you are living it."[4] It takes courage to live through our pain, but when we do, we are able to compassionately connect with and encourage others. If those who hurt see in you single-mindedness, sincerity and freedom from mixed motives—if they see your purity—they see a person to trust.

## NATALIE'S STORY

When I think of the pure in heart, Natalie immediately comes to mind. I first met her about twenty-five years ago as a student in the Bible Study Fellowship class I taught. Eventually she became a leader, and later she worked as a leader with me in a Life Design class.

Natalie has blonde hair, big blue eyes and a wide, open smile that seems to say, "I have time to talk. I hope you do too." She looks like one of the California girls the Beach Boys made famous. Never, given her outward presence, would you imagine the painful experiences she has faced.

Natalie is emphatic about not having the gift of evangelism. She's done extensive work on spiritual gifts and has identified exhortation, giving, service and helps as her primary gifts. Her vocational credo is "I exist to love people as they are and help them grow." That's how Natalie lives, and that's how she has brought many people to faith and supported them as they learned to serve Jesus as King within the fellowship of his church.

My question was, how did Natalie develop a pure heart? Everything she knew as a child worked against such a thing. She grew up in a family with a compulsively gambling, alcoholic father. Her grandfather taught him to drink and from adolescence on, liquor was his primary focus. In his occasional sober moments he was charming and generous, but such moments were rare. Mostly he shirked responsibility and reliability. He betrayed his family with broken promises and unabashed promiscuity. Eventually her father died a skid-row bum. Unfortunately, Natalie's mother's accumulated rage, and the chaos of their alcoholic household damaged everyone.

As is so often the case, Natalie repeated her mother's pattern. She married an alcoholic. Not surprisingly, that marriage failed. Soon after that she fell in love with Jim and married him. They shared similar backgrounds, but he was a cut above the other men she had known. When this marriage began to crumble, Natalie was desperate. At this point, her husband was out drinking every night with his friends while she was at home drinking herself into oblivion. One day a friend from work came to Natalie's home and told her that she had become a Christian. She was radiant.

A couple of weeks later Natalie went to her friend's baptism, and when she heard the testimonies of how Jesus filled the void in the lives of the people being baptized, she eagerly went forward to receive his salvation. She started studying the Bible right away, and as she grew in understanding, she identified and named four goals: to make her marriage work, to be a consistent and faithful wife and mother, to be an approachable person, and to bring respect and peace to every relationship and circumstance in her life.

Only when you know Natalie do you realize that behind each of these goals were agonizing pain and a great determination to break a destructive cycle. Recognizing the difficulty, Natalie nevertheless committed herself to do whatever it took to become a godly woman. She began to attend Bible studies, Al-Anon and anything else that supported her growth. She passionately pursued change as she lived a quiet life. She boldly faced all that fostered or threatened these four goals.

Her marriage was difficult. Jim felt that marriage was worth staying in only as long as it was working. When it didn't, well, you simply moved on. Natalie made it work. Jim noticed the change in her life. He would say that she was now "religious," but he didn't complain because the changes he saw benefited their family. Seventeen years later, through the consistency and purity of his wife, Jim met Jesus.

People noticed Jim and Natalie because they loved each other and their children. Many people enjoyed their friendship, but one person in particular watched them—their neighbor Jerry. Then, while only in his mid-fifties, Jim suffered a massive heart attack and died. The neighborhood women grew particularly close as they grieved with Natalie.

Jerry's live-in girlfriend, Linda, confided in Natalie, who had become a much-needed friend. Jerry was charming and handsome but undependable, Linda said. He had bad credit, he broke promises, and he was unfaithful to her. Yet he always promised to "go straight," and he was the only father her little Kathy knew, so she held onto his promise to marry her. Then Jerry impulsively married another woman and wanted to move his wife into the condo he owned with Linda.

Natalie helped Linda move to an affordable apartment, assisted in taking care of Kathy and comforted them both. Natalie was motivated and energized by love to help Linda. Dealing with Jerry, who was still her neighbor, proved a very different thing. Seeing him, even thinking of him, enraged her. Not only had he been emotionally cruel to Linda and Kathy, but he also managed to secure for himself two-thirds of the equity for the condo. Linda, who was barely scraping by, whose good credit had made the initial purchase possible, lost most of her investment in it after their nasty court battle.

When Jerry moved his new wife into the condo, Natalie's neighbors looked to her for an example of how to respond. She wondered herself. How could she, how could they, go on as if nothing had happened? Natalie knew the danger of grudges, but she was not emotionally prepared to forgive. She wanted to avoid the wife, and she wanted to hate Jerry. Then in the weekly Bible study she had with friends, she read Ephesians 4:25-27: "Therefore each of you must put off falsehood and speak truthfully to his neighbor, for we are all members of one body. 'In your anger do not sin': Do not let the sun

go down while you are still angry, and do not give the devil a foot-
hold."

God faithfully challenged her to review those four goals she had
created so long ago. Pure-in-heart woman that she is, she knew she
had to work through her anger. Slowly, prayerfully and tearfully, she
wrote Jerry a letter she intended never to send. She allowed it to
catch and absorb her anger. It helped her get it all out. Angry still, she
wrote again and again. With each draft there was improvement. In
the fourth letter the anger abated and communicated just the hurt
she felt. In that final letter she was able to "speak the truth in love"
(Eph 4:15) to Jerry. She boldly named the sins he committed and
spoke frankly of how his actions affected Kathy and Linda and, in
fact, all their friends in the neighborhood. Natalie admitted that it
was difficult to accept him back as a neighbor for these reasons.

She wisely sensed that a letter would allow Jerry time to face this
alone and to decide whether or not to respond. One morning she
placed the letter beneath his door and Jerry picked it up on his way
to work. Later that very morning, Natalie was startled by a loud
knock on her door. When she opened it, she saw Jerry, holding a large
briefcase bulging with papers. "I knew if there was anybody in the
neighborhood who had the guts to talk to me, it would be you," he
said.

It was obvious that Jerry had come to defend himself. In fact, all
the papers he carried pertained to his court case with Linda. Natalie
wisely rejected that direction of conversation and stayed with the
content of her own letter to him. She avoided all the justifying talk
and focused on the effects of Jerry's personal choices of betrayal,
abandonment, cowardice and financial slight-of-hand. In gentle honesty she confronted the many inconsistencies sprinkled throughout
their conversation. She spoke about the hurt so many people felt.

Gradually Jerry's defensive posture relaxed. He "just didn't get
it," but he wanted to. He really couldn't see why Linda and all her
friends were so hurt. He said he had made promises concerning
Linda and Kathy that he simply couldn't fulfill, and Natalie immedi-

ately stopped him. She pointed out what he was doing and held him to the truth, without anger, without disrespect. Finally Jerry said, "I just want to quit fighting. I just want peace."

Natalie said, "Jerry, forgiveness doesn't come quickly when you've been hurt deeply."

Who could know better than she that forgiveness is a process that goes far beyond mouthing the words, "I forgive you." This idea was a foreign concept to him, a reckless, middle-aged adult. For the first time in his life Jerry heard facts about forgiveness he had never heard before. He was like a little boy who had gotten into a big mess and had no idea how to get out of it.

Jerry showed his respect for Natalie and listened intently as she explained the necessity of forgiveness. For over an hour she unfolded the power of chastity, of single-mindedness, of sincerity, of living free of mixed motives—of a pure heart. He commented that he had watched Natalie and Jim's relationship, trying to figure out what made it so wonderful. She explained that they were Christians and that God had transformed their marriage and family. She shared the gospel and explained that when Jesus comes into our lives we experience God's forgiveness and, based on his forgiveness, we can forgive others. As of this writing, Jerry isn't ready to follow Jesus. However, now he knows what that means.

The first time I heard this story, I had two reactions. First I was amazed. God has a remarkable way of using Natalie's past to help her speak freedom to others. My second reaction was to realize that God gives opportunities like this to the pure of heart, to those who live for the praise of God and live without deceit, for inevitably this means they have the ability to help wounded people like Jerry and Linda. People wounded by sin know to trust them. Our families, our neighborhoods, our countries are filled with such wounded people. How willing are you to engage in the solitary refinement required for purity, which is so necessary to evangelism?

## ENGAGE IN BECOMING PURE IN HEART

1. What was helpful to you in this chapter?

2. How do you respond to the idea that suffering produces purity of heart?

3. Describe a time when you saw or experienced suffering that produced a genuine "vision of God." What happened to the people who went through this?

4. Paul's life is a model of how purity works in us and through us. Read his testimony of this in 1 Timothy 1:12-17.

    a. How can we know from this text that Paul lived primarily for the praise of God?

    b. What did Paul learn through the experience of being purified by God?

    c. How can you apply this text to your life?

5. Consider the non-Christians you are praying for. Examine how suffering in your life has purified you. How has your suffering prepared you to be a friend and witness to them?

6. Make an appointment with the unbelievers who might benefit from what you have experienced and learned. Approach these meetings with prayer. Ask God for a natural way to share your experiences. Record what happens as a result.

# 5
# BUOYANT

## JOINING THE
## GREAT COMMISSION CLUB

*They (early Christians) lived in a dangerous time. . . .*
*But it is hard to escape the impression that*
*in their day they lived buoyantly.*

THOMAS CAHILL

*I tell you the truth, anyone who has faith in me*
*will do what I have been doing. He will do even greater things*
*than these, because I am going to the Father.*
*And I will do whatever you ask in my name,*
*so that the Son may bring glory to the Father.*
*You may ask me for anything in my name, and I will do it.*

JOHN 14:12-14

**BUOYANCY** is that irresistible quality that puts
a smile on the face of perseverance. Our non-Christian friends are drawn to us because of it; and without it, evangelism becomes perfunctory, tedious
and often abandoned.

Buoyant wears a bright yellow vest. Any astute observer immediately gathers that she is not ordinary. Even on the darkest days she is smiling, laughing and gesturing for you to join her in the gentle pursuit of souls. If Buoyant belonged to a political party we would have to name it the Paradox Party—at least her speeches imply such. "Free!" she calls. Then she both cautions you to expect suffering and comforts you with the promise of joy. She speaks of restrained boldness and gentle power.

Those who are buoyant in evangelism are comfortable sharing what God is doing in their lives; and when they face opposition or resistance to the gospel, they remain respectful, focused and committed to their vocation. Buoyant may carry us out into rough seas where waves of discouragement wash over the side of our boat, but Buoyant stays with us, shouting over the gale, reminding us that the craft we're in is trustworthy.

Eugene Peterson interprets the Great Commission (Mt 28:18 The Message) this way: "Go out and train everyone you meet, far and near, in this way of life." When looking for the most apt word to describe how the first-century Christians engaged in the Great Commission (in the excerpt above), author Thomas Cahill settled on *buoyantly*. Sadly buoyancy (which might also be understood as joyful resilience) seems nearly as scarce now as rain is in the vast Sahara. Fewer and fewer believing adults in the Western world opt to obey the Great Commission. Missing are those core spiritual disciplines that accompany the commission. In my experience of training adults in evangelism, most Christians share their faith by witness and few evangelize.

It's time to intentionally bring buoyancy back to Christian character. Long enough we have languished like a beautiful boat with sails furled, heavy in the water and useless in the breeze. The Spirit waits to unfurl the sails and send us out to catch the strong breeze, to be safe, buoyant, useful, and beautiful on choppy seas.

## JESUS MAKES A PROMISE

On the night before he was crucified, Jesus—having spent three years training his disciples—said, "I tell you the truth, anyone who has faith in me will do what I have been doing. He will do even greater things than these, because I am going to the Father" (Jn 14:12). Jesus used the words *I tell you the truth* to draw the disciples' attention to the importance of what he was about to say.

Essentially he told them that when they believe not only would they do the same things he did, but they would do *greater* works. They would continue the work begun in the incarnation, the work of glorifying the Father through the Son. That is, "anyone who has faith . . . will" do these things.

The Greek word that Jesus used here for *believe* does not imply a superficial faith that takes an initial step but quits when the going gets rough. Nor does it imply a faith that believes only what is easy to believe and that gives up if what Jesus says conflicts with one's own ideas or plans. Instead, Jesus meant we must respond to what he said with commitment: with our mind, our heart and our behavior. To believe in him not as we would in another human being, like Gandhi or Buddha, but as the Son of God—the one who was crucified and resurrected on our behalf, the one always with us, the one who empowers us to fulfill his will. It is his promise that when we ask for anything that furthers God's cause, our request will be honored. Add to that the "greater thing"—God will honor the prayers of all believers who have this intention.

Another phenomenal promise in this text is that Jesus "will do whatever you ask in [his] name"(Jn 14:13). This doesn't mean that if we tack the phrase *in Jesus name* at the end of our prayers, Jesus will automatically answer them. Instead he promises that if we ask anything consistent with his character, Jesus will answer that prayer. Twice in this text he makes this promise: "You may ask me for anything in my name, and I will do it" (Jn 14:14).

Essentially, we find two promises in this text: "the one who believes in me will do even greater things than I do" and "ask me for anything in my name and I will do it." What could be clearer or more challenging?

A pastor once told his congregation, "I have some good news and some unsettling news for you. The good news is that we have all the money we need to build our new facility. The unsettling news is that it's in your pockets." Jesus said a similar thing about evangelism.

The good news from Jesus is that he "came to seek and to save what was lost" (Lk 19:10). The unsettling news (especially for shy or busy believers) is that he is going to use us to do it. Today he uses us to do the seeking. He provides all the resources we need to engage in evangelism. This does not mean evangelism will be easy. We live in a world awash with the power of Satan (1 Jn 5:19). Our very own culture is dominated by the enemy's message of self-indulgence and independence, which is powerfully opposed to the gospel. Satan does everything he can to keep people in a state of unbelief, including discouraging Christians from evangelizing.

It isn't too difficult for many of us to say a few words about our experience with God to our unbelieving friends. But when it comes to enduring in a long-term relationship with an unbeliever and loving her or him unconditionally while maintaining an evangelistic focus, witnessing on an increasingly deep level that eventually opens the door for the gospel to be relevant, and offering our friend the opportunity to receive Christ—well, then we are tempted to look at the crowded calendar, review our long "to do" list, give thanks for our friends who "have the gift" and shy away from evangelism.

## BUOYANCY IN MOTION

When we think of living a Great Commission lifestyle and have the focus it requires, we're more apt to stay afloat if we attach our mission to a symbol we can picture when the going gets rough. I carry a swimmer's kick-board in my mind. I promise you there will be dark days when sticking with the Great Commission Club will be difficult. Maintaining buoyancy in evangelism means having hope, regardless of how things look, that God is at work and that he will not give up for he doesn't want any to perish (2 Pet 3:9).

Everything I know about buoyancy I learned from using a pool buoy. I swim for conditioning. For about five minutes of my freestyle warm-up, the pool buoy keeps my legs on the surface and stores in my body the memory of correct positioning so that when I remove the buoy and swim, my legs stay near the top of the water. Next in my workout I spend a few minutes on the kick-board, where buoyant legs are essential to swimming fast and efficiently. With my body rightly aligned, I can swim a mile without being exhausted. Usually I feel like I could keep swimming indefinitely. What pushes me out of the water is the tedium of counting laps!

A friend of mine who has been a swimmer for many years has never used a pool buoy. Not so long ago she saw me warming up, first with the buoy then five minutes with the kick-board. She confided that all her attempts at using the kick-board were frustrating. "I just don't go anywhere," she sighed. She asked me to watch her swim and comment on what it was about her form that prevented her from being efficient with the kick-board. The problem was immediately apparent. She swims almost vertically. She gets a great upper body workout but her legs are next to useless. As we talked about it, the problem became clear to her, but it was too much trouble to change her old habits.

As Christians, don't we often feel just that way? We cling to the old comfortable way, even though we aren't as effective as we know we could be.

Evangelism is not possible without buoyancy. I wouldn't be writing this book and you wouldn't be reading it if the earliest Christians had not been buoyant. They didn't go under when the going got tough. They didn't surrender to despair when people they loved walked away from faith. Unsinkable in hope, they kept on, and many of those who first refused the good news eventually turned to Christ.

## EVANGELISM: A GIFT AND A ROLE

Some people have the uncanny ability to proclaim the good news and see people who are ready to receive it. They have the gift, no doubt about it. They proclaim the gospel and people pray to receive Christ. People with the recognizable spiritual gift of evangelism represent a small percentage of the church population. Their gift is more than just leading people to Christ. They also give to Christians who aren't gifted in evangelism the insights they gather from their experiences. For example, I have greatly benefited from the teaching and writings of Rebecca Pippert, Joseph Aldrich and others. Evangelists share insights and experiences with the rest of us, and we learn evangelism skills that can be expressed through our own gifts.

Imagine that you work in an office by day and participate in family duties around the clock, but because you love acting, you are also a cast member of the little theater in your town. You assume a role: you learn the part well and present it effectively. It becomes easy and pleasurable, but it is not *you*. Your primary role is elsewhere. Now consider the difference it might make if we finally acknowledged the truth that many people come to faith in Jesus through ordinary Christians who don't have the gift of evangelism but who have learned to effectively assume the role of an evangelist.

When we read Paul's lists of spiritual gifts in Romans 12, 1 Corinthians 12 and Ephesians 4, we find that many gifts are simply behaviors all Christians are expected to engage in, even if we are not "spiritually gifted" in these areas. For example, all of us are called to be merciful, and some of us have the gift of mercy. All of us are called to help each other, and some of us have the gift of helps. All Christian parents have the responsibility to teach their children about basic Christian beliefs and practices. Only a few of these parents are spiritually gifted to teach a Sunday school class. I know I don't have the spiritual gift of miracles, yet I regularly experience miraculous answers to my prayers.

I work for Life Design, an outreach ministry that includes Bible study and elective classes that teach practical living skills and creative crafts. Every year we have the opportunity to train our Life Design leaders in evangelism skills. Most are gifted in other areas, but they are committed to bringing people to Jesus and training them to serve him as King. The one thing that excites our leaders beyond all else is participating in the conversion of the unbelievers who attend Life Design. I have found it universally true that evangelism brings an excitement to Christians that comes in no other way—whether they serve in a role or with a gift.

## WHAT CREATES BUOYANCY IN EVANGELISM?

After the resurrection and the coming of the Holy Spirit, Christians were identified as those "who belonged to the Way" (Acts 9:2). They followed the Lord so closely that the "way" they were doing things was as Jesus did. By reading the New Testament we recognize the distinct personalities of individual Christians, but we also find some strong common experiences among them that enabled them to be buoyant.

*Encounter with Christ.* Over and over again we find that followers of Jesus each had an encounter with the risen Christ inspiring enough to transform their lives. Three days after the resurrection two despairing disciples were walking to Emmaus. They had set their hope on Jesus' redemption of Israel, setting it free from Roman rule. They had heard rumors of his resurrection, but since they had not yet seen Jesus, these reports did little more than create confusion.

Then Jesus joined them on that road. Luke tells us their eyes were kept from seeing Jesus. As was the Lord's habit, he inquired about their situation. When they explained their predicament to Jesus, Luke says "he explained to them what was said in all the Scriptures concerning himself" (Lk 24:27). Later the disciples described the event, saying, "Were not our hearts burning within us while he talked with us on the road and opened the Scriptures to us?" (Lk 24:32). An encounter with Christ inspires transformation, and that transformation marks us as people of the Way. Every generation of Christians for twenty-one centuries has told its story of experiencing the risen Christ in undeniable ways. Buoyancy in evangelism stems from a vital experience of meeting with Jesus.

*Empowerment of the Holy Spirit.* Buoyancy must also be described as a characteristic of the Holy Spirit. What else accounts for the dramatic transformation of Peter? If ever there was an image of a swimmer with his body vertical in the pool, Peter is it. On the night before Jesus was crucified, Peter was unable to resist the temptation to deny his connection to Jesus. Seven weeks later, on the day of Pentecost, the Holy Spirit came into Peter and other disciples who were waiting and praying for his promised arrival. These disciples remembered that Jesus said the Holy Spirit would reside within them: they would never be alone. The Spirit would give them power and boldness to witness. He would convict unbelievers of their sin. He would comfort the disciples in whatever way they needed it. He would teach them everything about Jesus they needed to know. And he would guide them in all truth.

These men and women were familiar with the power of Jesus, and they recognized their inability to live as he did. They wanted God's Spirit enough to pray and wait for him to come and live inside of them. The sudden indwelling of the Holy Spirit is the only thing that accounts for how Peter—an uneducated, fearful fisherman—was able to boldly preach his first sermon to thousands of devout Jews. As a result, on the day of Pentecost, three thousand people repented from their sins and received God's forgiveness and his Holy Spirit. The believing church, then and now, stands on the gospel and stays afloat by the indwelling Holy Spirit. Without his empowering presence we might as well be swimming in molasses. His power is the buoyant lift in evangelism.

*Engaging in spiritual disciplines.* Buoyancy comes through the practice of certain spiritual disciplines, such as prayer, fasting, meeting with other believers and Bible reading. When we read the Acts account of how early disciples lived after Pentecost, we realize how rightfully this account might have been titled "Buoyancy in Action":

> They devoted themselves to the apostles' teaching and to the fellowship, to the breaking of bread and to prayer. Everyone was filled with awe, and many wonders and miraculous signs were done by the apos-

tles. All the believers were together and had everything in common. Selling their possessions and goods, they gave to anyone as he had need. Every day they continued to meet together in the temple courts. They broke bread in their homes and ate together with glad and sincere hearts, praising God and enjoying the favor of all the people. And the Lord added to their number daily those who were being saved. (Acts 2:42-47)

It must have been wonderful. First these Christians were diligent in hearing the authentic teaching of Jesus as it came directly from the apostles—those followers Jesus taught, trained and commissioned to spread the gospel of God's grace. Converts drawn from every quarter of society listened, learned and let others know what was happening. They ardently engaged in Christian fellowship. They were unified in their beliefs. Each one sought the risen Lord for guidance and for strength to fulfill the Great Commission, and they experienced his unfailing faithfulness. Whether it was by martyrdom or miracle, that early band of believers prospered under the protection of spiritual disciplines. Imagine the intensity of it all. It seems a far cry from what many of us experience during fellowship time at our church social hours!

Being Jews, these early Christians were intimately familiar with the ritual cleansings necessary according to religious law. Amazingly, at his last supper Jesus used the cup and the bread to bring new meaning to familiar elements. Regularly and faithfully they remembered Christ's body and blood shed to make it possible for them to experience God's forgiveness. "Do this . . ." Jesus said (Lk 22:19). And they did, and we do. We discipline ourselves to remember the difference of that which had been before and that which is now—now that we know Jesus.

They were dedicated also to attending the common prayer of Jews in the temple. Thomas Cahill writes that

> the centerpiece of synagogue prayer was the reading from the sacred scrolls of scripture, which the Messianists heard as now-obvious prophecies of their Christ, so that this prayer branched out for them in

two directions, confirming both their Jewish identity and their new insight into its previous hidden meaning.[1]

The Gentile believer Luke is responsible for much of the New Testament writings. In Acts, which was written during the first century A.D., he shows how Christians lived during the first thirty years or so after the resurrection. He exposes a time when Christian faith was threatened both from within by growing false doctrines and from without by aggressive Jewish opposition and persecution and by fierce, official threats from Rome, which by this time, was feeling the enormous impact of Christian faith. Reading Luke's account, we learn what it takes to bring people to Christ. I find it comforting, even amazing, that every generation has struggled under the difficulty in walking out the Great Commission.

Spiritual disciplines, far from restricting the followers of Jesus, freed them and gave them over to glad and generous hearts. Their priorities were upended, their motives were refreshed, and their duty turned to desire. Luke explains that awe came upon everyone, including nonbelievers, as early Christians engaged in seeking God, committed themselves to the guidance and power of the Holy Spirit, maintained spiritual disciplines and practiced evangelism.

We see around us many examples of corporate greed and corruption. We wag our heads over the selfishness of the wealthy clamoring for more wealth. But we have also read of wealthy business owners who have generously exhausted their own wealth to care for their employees in times of distress. How we marvel at such rare acts of compassion! In the first century the reaction to such kindness was no different. The Christians' generosity and their efforts to meet others' needs caused the community around them to marvel. Ministry was just as Jesus had promised: in the collective sense, they did even greater things than Jesus; and together they were able to glorify the Father in a manner that far surpassed what any one of them could have done alone.

What are we to make of this today? Certainly effective first-century Christians were focused in their mission. They were disciplined in worship and prayer, both privately and corporately. Their community thrived on their shared experiences of Jesus, his mandate and their own resources. If we find ways today to obey the call of God to express such corporate caring, the community around us will be as curious as were those who watched the first generation of the church. And they will be as responsive. Our world longs for what Jesus has given us. But we must share it. There is no magical path to developing glad and generous hearts or to participating in saving souls. There is only discipline.

When I teach on this, I often hear people in the audience groan. These simple directives from the Lord fly in the face of how most Christians live. Too often the complexity and urgency of our routines prevent us from experiencing the depth and breadth of God's love that we find as we walk out his Great Commission. We who purpose to fulfill its mandate must carefully assess and evaluate our priorities. We must care about being deliberate in a careless culture. We must be quick to ask, "What is of God?" For what we do with time and with people matters in God's eternal scheme, not just in our personal planners.

In Scripture I discover God's priorities, and they change my plans as I grow spiritually. I find it easier to discern God's intent in Scripture now than I did twenty or thirty years ago. It's much easier for me to evaluate whether what I'm presently doing fits with my Great Commission focus. I anticipate more growth year by year.

## STEPHANIE'S STORY

When I was a new Christian, it was "religiously correct" in my circle of believers to think of the world as totally dark and of the unconverted as the "enemy." While Scripture gives some reason for that viewpoint, it also gives evidence to the contrary. For instance, I think of a man like King Abimelech of Gerar who lived more righteously than Abraham, who lied to him (Gen 20). In the New Testament we find Cornelius, a Roman centurion, whom Luke describes this way: "He and all his family were devout and God-fearing; he gave generously to those in need and prayed to God regularly" (Acts 10:2). And this was before Cornelius became a Christian. These Gentile men were faithful to the light they had. They represent many good people today: people who are not yet believers, often because nobody has shown them Jesus, either by word or by the example of character; sometimes because their personal integrity requires that they wait for genuine conviction.

Of course, we have valuable things to offer our seeking friends. Paul gives us a list of them: "love, joy, peace, patience, kindness, goodness, faithfulness, gentleness and self-control" (Gal 5:22). But we are often challenged by friendships with people who live more like Christ than many believers do. I have learned a lot about buoyancy in evangelism through my friendship with Stephanie.

Stephanie is one of those noble people who has not yet become a Christian. Usually when we hear the word *noble* we think of famous or memorable people like Mother Teresa, Pope John Paul, Jimmy Carter or Billy Graham. At the top of my list stands Stephanie. At thirty-two she is wiser than most her age. She's a woman of integrity, as beautiful on the inside as she is on the outside, which is saying a lot. She's honest to the point of declaring her tips on taxes. She is a parent extraordinaire and the sort of friend most of us long to have (and be).

I met Stephanie when I hired her to train my dog. I knew nothing about her except her reputation as a dog trainer and her ad in the yellow pages. I frequently took my yellow lab, Carmel, to her for training. Carmel needed it and her need offered me opportunity to build a friendship with Stephanie. I doubt that I talked much about God at first. After all, I was paying Stephanie to perform a service for me. One day, out of the blue, she said, "Chris, I know you do public speaking. I hope I can come hear you one day because I really respect you." I was flabbergasted.

A few months later I had a speaking engagement on a Saturday, so I invited Stephanie. She was unable to attend but wanted to know about my topic. When she heard I was speaking on relationships, she told me, "I wish I wasn't working so I could come. I need to learn about relationships. My mom's been married three times, and my husband's mother, four. My husband and I just don't know how to do this." There, in that moment that I believe God arranged, she began to tell me about her disappointment with marriage.

As she talked about it, an idea came to mind. "Stephanie," I offered, "Don and I have been married for thirty-five years. Would it be helpful to you if we met once a week to talk about building a good marriage? I know you exercise and so do I. What if we walk while we talk?"

"I would love that, Chris, but I know you want me to stay married, and I don't know if it's going to come out that way." She sighed heavily. "I don't want to disappoint you or waste your time."

"I don't have an agenda for our talks," I assured her. "You are an adult and I believe in you. You have demonstrated wisdom to me many times. I can offer you a healthy perspective on marriage. I can tell you how Don and I worked through similar rough spots, if you ask. I am willing to be a sounding board. What do you think?"

Under these conditions, Stephanie welcomed the opportunity to walk and talk with me. While it was true that I didn't have an agenda for our time together, it was also true that Stephanie knew that my faith influenced how I interpreted life. She intuitively understood our conversations would include God. She also knew I would not ignore or minimize the human or relational issues she was facing. After meeting for a couple of weeks, we decided to read the book *Men Are from Mars, Women Are from Venus* by John Gray.

*Men Are from Mars, Women Are from Venus* presents the very different approaches men and women take to life and their relationships. It's a book about the human aspects of gender that add to or detract from a healthy marriage. Stephanie and I went through most of it, one chapter a week.

I don't remember who chose the book, but it was one Stephanie was comfortable with and that was of primary importance. Evangelism requires that we approach unbelievers where they are, not where we want them to be so that they feel safe enough to share what is really going on with them. I simply wanted to listen to her and help her gain basic insights into relationships between men and women. She wanted my response.

I had many opportunities to offer spiritual observations. In the year we walked together, I often talked about how God helped Don and me through hard times. Whenever she reached a crisis in her home, I offered to pray right then for God to intervene. Stephanie wanted and appreciated my prayers. I prayed as we kept walking. It was hard and sometimes tedious work for both of us. Looking back, I marvel that Stephanie stuck with it.

Stephanie received valuable insight from the book, and she tried hard to make her marriage work. When after great effort it didn't work, she faced the ramifications divorce would have on her husband, their son and herself. Before getting married, she swore she would never get divorced. She struggled and she cried many tears. When finally she came to the understanding that even with all the consequences a divorce was necessary, I knew it was not a reckless decision. I could counsel her, but the decision was hers and hers alone. She looked carefully ahead to forty or fifty years of life under her present conditions and couldn't choose to stay married.

Stephanie's desire to protect her family and maintain privacy deprived all but a very few of the truth in her own situation. Some of Stephanie's Christian friends—who intended well but were largely uninformed about the pertinent psychological issues and the thorough approach Stephanie took before deciding on divorce—were more of a hindrance than a help during this time. They offered her judgmental sermons. They gave her advice. Listening was not a priority to them, nor did they measure the appropriateness or effect of their message in this particular situation. There is no buoyancy in such a heavy-handed approach.

During the months before the divorce became final, Stephanie went to a Bible study, where she learned more accurately what a Christian is. At this point my witnessing finally turned into evangelism. She and I seriously talked about Jesus during this time. She had two strong areas of resistance. The first came from her Mormon background: she could not yet accept that Jesus was God. This was one of her ingrained beliefs. Aside from that, she now faced an even greater hurdle: she didn't want to be affiliated with the Christian church because she saw it as her mother experienced the Mormon church—narrow and judgmental. She appreciates those Christians who understand the complexities she faced, but she doesn't see their behavior as the norm. I see her point. Too often I've experienced narrow and judgmental behavior in the church. On the other hand, God has blessed her in ways that she can clearly see.

At this writing, Stephanie just isn't ready to commit to Jesus. In fact, the closer she gets, the harder she pulls away from Christianity. I was not surprised when she herself acknowledged that. I realized that my response to her confession was as important as anything I've ever said or done for her. During the year and a half of our friendship, we had grown to love each other deeply. I was sad and disappointed by her decision. I also meant to receive it with the very grace God means for me to share. I told her that I would continue to pray for her and that this needn't change our relationship. I knew that decisions about spirituality finally belonged between Stephanie and God.

When Stephanie faltered so close to the kingdom, I found it difficult to remain buoyant, to keep living the Great Commission lifestyle. I began questioning my own representation of Jesus, and I wanted to rail against the tactics of other Christians. I was casting about for something or someone to blame, really. I was frustrated by the Christians who judged her, and I was frustrated for myself, or maybe it is more honest to say, sorry for myself. I asked myself, *Having invested so much time and energy, was it really worth it?* Of course I wondered whether I should have done something differently.

Then I realized that my relationship with Stephanie is so honest that she would have told me if her struggle was with my representation of Jesus. I have to accept that her battle is with God. I turned my attention to my own spiritual disciplines, to recognizing that my work is to do what Jesus did—glorify the Father. I can help lead people to the Savior, but I am not the Savior. As I prayed for the strength to find my proper place in this amazing drama of evangelism, I began to experience God lifting my spirits. I began to find the buoyancy I needed to persevere in my relationship with Stephanie and others despite any disappointment.

### Overcoming the Weakness of Relational Evangelism

The sort of evangelism I've described here (it may be called one-on-one evangelism, lifestyle evangelism or even friendship evangelism) has a weak point: as the friendship between a believer and a nonbeliever grows, the emphasis can easily become genuine friendship while neglecting genuine evangelism. My goal was to bring Stephanie to faith in Christ. It was powerfully tempting to give up on evangelizing her, yet God's Great Commission mandates that we remain focused on making disciples.

It is in situations like this that the symbol of the swimmer's kickboard helps. Buoyancy keeps us afloat spiritually. Before the meeting in the office begins, before the luncheon, before the walk and before the telephone conversation, we are privileged to call on the Holy Spirit, asking that he properly position our thoughts and intentions, our focus. In the years since I first started meeting with Stephanie, we have maintained a loving friendship. We still talk about spiritual things. Recently she called me with an urgent prayer request. I see signs that God is continuing to draw her to Jesus.

How long will it be before Stephanie believes in Jesus? Will she ever come to faith? I don't have answers for those questions. But I know this: God is faithfully drawing her to himself. Have I given up on my responsibility to love her "in Jesus' name" or to keep refining the spiritual disciplines that prepare me for representing the Lord? I have not and dare not. Buoyancy keeps me going even when the path is difficult.

## ENGAGE IN BECOMING BUOYANT

1. What is most noteworthy to you in this chapter?

2. What do you see as your opportunities for growth in developing buoyancy in evangelism?

3. Read aloud the story of Paul and Silas in Troas (Acts 16:16-34). Read it slowly and try to imagine what these men actually experienced.

   a. Identify several challenges to staying buoyant Paul and Silas faced.

   b. How is the way they faced these challenges reflected in this chapter on being buoyant?

   c. Review the character qualities you have read in previous chapters. How do Paul and Silas reflect each one?

   d. Describe the effect of this episode on the jailer.

   e. What to you is the most important point of this story?

4. Why do you think hardship plays a role in the development of buoyancy?

# 6
## WISE

### WHEN ALL ELSE FAILS, READ THE DIRECTIONS

*The world has more winnable people than ever before . . .*
*but it is possible to come out of a ripe field empty-handed.*

DONALD MCGAVRAN

*As Jesus was walking beside the Sea of Galilee,*
*he saw two brothers, Simon called Peter and his brother Andrew.*
*They were casting a net into the lake,*
*for they were fishermen.*
*"Come, follow me," Jesus said, "and I will make you fishers of men."*

MATTHEW 4:18-19

**WISDOM** is knowing the right thing to do and then doing it. We gain wisdom through our experiences with evangelism, and we are wise to apply patience to this process.

Among members of my family I'm notorious for failing to read directions before I use a new product. This approach has worked so well with uncomplicated appliances that any suggestion of change has fallen on deaf ears—mine. For ten years the owner's manual to my car has been tucked in the glove compartment, untouched and unnecessary. I figure I don't need it to drive the car but will use it if and when a problem arises. That time came at a recent visit to the Department of Motor Vehicles. When the license examiner requested that I locate the hazard lights button for him, I couldn't. I admitted at that point that it might have been wise for me to have checked the page showing the dashboard display when we first purchased my car. This time came again when, with my arms full of things I was carrying into the Salvation Army store, I kicked my car door closed and my car screamed in response. The alarm system suddenly howled, piercing the serenity of an early Tuesday morning. When the wailing refused my pleas to stop, I did what I knew I should have done: I reached for the owner's manual. But before the pages were opened the alarm stopped as suddenly as it had begun. I quickly tucked the unread manual back into the glove compartment, finished unloading my car and, in blissful silence, started for home. Three short blocks from my house, the car alarm sounded off again. I will admit to this: had I at any time in ten years read the manual, this would not have happened—at least it would not have happened twice.

Twenty-some years ago I attended a Christian conference where Donald McGavran was teaching an elective class on church planting. I knew little about this respected man, but I soon found that his grasp on the necessities of evangelism and his expertise on church planting were stunning. For all his credentials and scholarly insight, he captured and challenged me with this simple statement: "If you want to be a successful fisherman, go to where the fish are biting!" If we want to fish for people, McGavran said, we must return to Scripture, the source that shows us how it's done.

Proverbs tells us that those who actually win souls are wise (Prov 11:30). Interestingly, wisdom is a spiritual gift for some, yet all Christians are called to walk in wisdom. Wisdom is a partnership between knowledge and experience. Jesus increased in wisdom, and so can we (Lk 2:52). Developing wisdom requires first that we know something and then that we rightly apply that knowledge and grow through the experience of application. One who is wise is not primarily concerned with getting a particular result, for though success may follow wise action, it is not the proof of it. Fools and thugs may be successful, but they are not wise. The plans of the wise may fail, but their character will not. These principles are applicable to evangelism. Keep in mind that the very sequence of knowledge, application and experience welcomes trial and error. The model of fishing Jesus gave us illustrates this.

### LEARNING TO FISH FROM JESUS

One day Jesus stood at the shore of the Sea of Galilee and watched two fishermen, Peter and Andrew, cast their net into the water. Jesus was thinking of a special band of men he would train as his apprentices, and he meant to include Peter and Andrew. Jesus wisely addressed them with language they understood: "Come, follow me, and I will make you fishers of men." From there, Matthew records their amazing response: "At once they left their nets and followed him" (Mt 4:19-20).

Several others among Jesus' first disciples were Galilean fishermen. When he pointed them toward fishing for people, they immediately and fully understood his intention. Their understanding was instantaneous because Jesus spoke their language and used an image they could grasp. (The ancient art of fishing has much to offer those of us still learning.)[1] However, the record shows that putting their knowledge into practice took time. It took these disciples three years of being with Jesus to learn how to transfer the skills of catching deep-water fish to catching dry-land people.

In biblical times fishermen worked in teams and with nets. The most important net used in the Sea of Galilee was the *siene,* or as it is more commonly called, the dragnet. For this kind of fishing the deck was loaded with a huge net, some sinkers, floats and ropes. The dragnet—250 to 300 meters long and three to four meters high—had rope sewn at the top and at the bottom. Lead sinkers pulled the bottom rope to the sea floor while cork floats kept the top rope buoyant on the sea's surface.

Mendel Nun, in his book *The Sea of Galilee and Its Fishermen in the New Testament,* describes what happens next.

> In the early morning the crew . . . sails off to "catch" a good fishing area. When . . . the boat touches shore, half the crew alight and take the first rope. The boat sails out . . . until it reaches the end of the line. The boat then turns and sails parallel to the shore until the net is "spread." The boat then turns back to the shore trailing the second set of ropes. On reaching the shore, the remaining half of the crew alights and takes the end of the other towing line, leaving the boat "detained" on the shore.
>
> The whole team now . . . pull[s] the net to the shore. The sinkers have dragged the net to the bottom, the floats have lifted the head-rope and the net now forms a rectangular wall that advances to the shore with its lower edge at the bottom of the lake. The . . . fishermen climb from the water up the beach, moving . . . toward each other. The seine method utilizes the nature of fish to dive to the bottom and to try to escape toward the deep water when they are in danger. Thus the fish in the space surrounded by the dragnet are caught.[2]

Nun explains that a good catch can weigh up to hundreds of kilos. The very weight of the catch threatens to break the nets, so one fisherman's task was to remain in the boat, making occasional dives to repair tears or to release bottom snags. The process of fishing one spot from start to finish took about an hour and was repeated up to eight times a day. And so we learn that tenacity, time and repeated efforts are part of the work of fishing—and of evangelism.

It is also important for us to realize that not all fishermen worked the same system. There are several ways to fish the Sea of Galilee. Some nets are small enough for a single person to handle either from the shore or casting from a boat. When I was at the conference where McGavran was teaching, I was glad to hear that bit of news. I was the only woman at the weekend conference, and it seemed to me that fishermen need to be strong, brawny and, well, masculine. I fail in all counts, if compared to men. However, I was encouraged to learn of differing fishing styles, of stuff that came as naturally to me as it did to my male colleagues. I could easily learn the nature of fish, the depth of the water, the best time to fish for various types of fish, the nature of currents and the sea floor and how to read the waters. I know how to swim and I appreciate the many challenges of team-work. Every step of their ancient fishermen's experience corre-sponded to some essential skill necessary to evangelism, and I rejoiced that those skills did not exclude me.

Let me present another image, a new way of looking at God's work of fishing for people. For some marvelous and mysterious rea-son, our Lord has chosen to enlarge his kingdom through us. He hon-ors each of us by giving us the role of evangelist. After twenty centuries the principles of evangelism Jesus demonstrated and passed on to the church prove timeless. Even if we're working with a small net and fishing in our own little cove, the truth is that when we're pulling in people for God's kingdom, we are working a line with other believers. It's all a part of a larger catch that covers years and great distances and that involves a number of other people hold-ing some part of the rope.

If you are the first person to witness to an unbeliever, then you're the first on the line. Maybe ten years go by and that person now lives a thousand miles away from you; God brings someone else to wit-ness—the second person to pull on the line. Who knows how many others have tugged or repaired that net between the time you threw it out, giving the unbeliever room to climb in, and when he or she ac-tually receives Jesus. Wise are those who realize that evangelism is a team effort and that God puts the team together as surely as Jesus did.

The truth of teamwork did not slip past the apostle Paul, who wrote:

> I planted the seed, Apollos watered it, but God made it grow. So neither he who plants nor he who waters is anything, but only God, who makes things grow. The man who plants and the man who waters have one purpose. . . . For we are God's fellow workers. (1 Cor 3:6-9)

We can argue that our problem is that not everyone on our team does a good job. Apollos and Paul were outstanding, but our coevangelists are not of the same caliber as they. We have (to continue the fishing metaphor) some long-standing bad fishing habits among us. Our cultural waters are polluted by stagnant, prepackaged "spiritual" (even Christian) opportunities to evangelize. Many of us know people with tales of being happily "hooked" by the gospel only to be carelessly tossed to the bottom of the boat by the zealous fisherman who turns back to catching his limit. There's little chance of growth or life at the bottom of a boat. There's little hope for those who have been roughly brought in and then thrown back, injured and alone. We must add wisdom to our tackle box.

Before we ever put our hands to the net we must first heed Jesus' prerequisite command, "Follow me." Following implies a lasting relationship between apprentice and teacher. A follower of Jesus is one whose life is redirected in obedience to him. Wisdom comes as a result of gaining God's perspective on life. In order to do so, we must follow him.

What did Jesus mean when he said, "Come, follow me, and I will make you fishers of men"? It is likely that Jesus said this to his disciples with the authority of a call and a contagious spirit. In today's vernacular we might hear it this way, "If you will hang in and follow where I go and do what I do, then *before you know it*, you'll be evangelizing people." The disciples liked Jesus. They enjoyed being with him. He was so amazing, he had such admirable qualities, that they were inspired to leave their fishing nets and follow him full-time! We learn from Isaiah that the Messiah, Jesus, drew people by his inner qualities rather than by slick or clever devices (Is 53:2).

Since this is Jesus' main point, we should investigate what he meant by "make." The verb Jesus uses means "to act" and applies to all activity. Dallas Willard picked up the intent of what Jesus said when he concluded, "True Christlikeness, true companionship with Christ, comes at the point where it is hard not to respond as he would."[3]

During a church leadership training course for an evangelistic outreach, one of our pastors asked us to list some reasons why Christians find evangelism difficult. We had no trouble coming up with the usual reasons: we think we don't know enough, we're too busy, we're afraid people will be put off. We came up with many reasons to be inhibited. When we turned back to Matthew 4:19—"Come, follow me, and I will make you fishers of men"—we discovered that if we follow Jesus, then we can't help but evangelize. Don't we wish it were as simple as that!

I find that unless we are exceptionally disciplined, we will struggle with following the Lord on a path of evangelizing. We may have to do some talking to ourselves, as I'm guessing some of the original disciples did. *What do I want to do more than anything? I want to follow him. But what about this boat, these nets, this business, my fear of speaking, my family obligations? What if he says sell, walk away, trust me, bring them along, change? Do I mean it when I say I want to follow?* Our heart's desire to follow has to silence our objections. From the beginning the Spirit teaches us to love him with our minds and hearts, and he prepares us to walk where Jesus walks. So first, we must realize that God goes before us, preparing the way. We have to trust that the gospel is the "wisdom of God" to save people (1 Cor 1:18-21). Then, with these truths as our foundation, we only have to cooperate—show up and walk through the doors Jesus will open; attentively use our hands, eyes and ears; and eventually open our mouths to speak of who Jesus is and what he means to us.

Don't let fear hold you back. I've never met Christians more excited about God and more deeply in love with people than those who are following his command to fish. Jesus certainly expressed this deep satisfaction after his encounter with the Samaritan woman. What was true for Jesus soon became true for his earliest followers and is true for us today: evangelism brings a deep spiritual satisfaction found no other way.

Jesus offers us the opportunity to follow and partner with him in life-giving conversations at work, at home, in our neighborhoods and anywhere else we may go. We might not yet see ourselves as adept or powerful communicators—we may feel foolish struggling to toss that heavy net—but Jesus is skilled and he works alongside us. He is the master fisherman, teaching us what and where and how and when. Because he is with us, we are to fish. Ordinary events and ordinary people become interesting or even approachable when we trust in him. These people become important to us as they are to God, as subjects of eternity.

## EVANGELISM THEN AND NOW

As we begin this journey of wise evangelism, the initial step is familiar: we follow Jesus to the place where fish can be found. We may be surprised then, once there, that Jesus isn't necessarily traditional in his approach to his work—and by association, we need not be. Jesus had an uncanny understanding of the issues belonging to the first-century Israelites (political, social, emotional, mental and spiritual) and shaped his ministry accordingly. Frequently in conversations he used contemporary issues and items as teaching tools. When was the last time you transitioned from the topic of taxes to the topic of faith? He did. He presented a distinct and lively theology by sticking to truth but applying it to the pressing concerns of his audience. He looked out at the crowds and understood that they suffered under oppressive governments, both foreign and local. Clearly, with compassion and relevance, he addressed that situation by addressing the basic human need—the leadership of God in an individual's life.

In an era of global distress, people today crave substantive spiritual food. Like Jesus in his day, we must be aware of and sensitive to current issues that provide new approaches to evangelism. If our traditional ways are not effective, then we must lay them aside. It takes courage and effort to embrace the people in this world with unconditional love as Jesus did. It takes wisdom. We need to learn how Jesus approached people then so we can do it now as he did.

*A bit of history.* The biblical scholars I have studied with in Israel call their country "the land in between." It stands between the continents of Europe, Asia and Africa. When Jesus walked the earth, caravans from these continents regularly passed through Israel. Nazareth, the town where Jesus spent his childhood, is situated atop a ridge overlooking the valley crisscrossed by those rutted, well-worn roads. It's likely that as a growing boy, Jesus watched those caravans; perhaps he even interacted with the travelers and learned from them. During the years of his ministry the Romans occupied Israel, bringing with them pagan worship, heavy taxes and a general disdain for the Jews. In short, it is accurate to say that Jesus was going to teach his disciples how to throw nets into a sea filled with a surprising variety of "fish."

The people of Israel enjoyed traditions that had changed little over the centuries. The tools they used, the clothes they wore and the beliefs they held were, in most respects, identical to those of their ancestors. Like all entrenched habits, some of these were richly rewarding and some dangerously stagnant. Imagine, then, how threatening it must have been for people to hear something seemingly new from Jesus—a theology, a teaching that explained the significance of law by relaxing it and that summed up justice in the word *grace*. In the end it proved threatening enough for the nation's leaders to call for Jesus' crucifixion.

Like the leaders in many societies, Jewish leaders were divided into various parties jockeying for power and control and were riddled with schisms. The strongest two sects at that time were the Pharisees and the Sadducees. They had predictable differences; their spats were "traditional" and familiar. But the challenge Jesus brought to the arguments at hand forced a belief gap humanly impossible to bridge. Ordinary people were caught in this gap. Average citizens knew the value of keeping clear of the leaders; they knew the value of maintaining the status quo—not only to please the local leaders, but also to stave off any aggression from Rome. Following Jesus threatened the *pax,* the enforced peace, both public and private.

Actually, the majority of people who followed Jesus knew no *pax.* A few upper-class Jews were among his close group of followers, but generally speaking those who willingly listened to the Lord were anxious. They were the poor, the harassed, the helpless. They had no power and little protection from either local or foreign leaders. Truly they were, as Jesus described, "sheep without a shepherd" (Mk 6:34). They squirmed under the heels of various powers largely disinterested in their plight. The mob; those at the bottom of the barrel emotionally, physically, economically; those with little to lose and much to gain—these are the ones who came to Jesus. Little has changed. Some people are miserable with how their lives are, and they are ready to follow Jesus. They want to relish his wisdom and be touched by his compassion. Still, in the time of Jesus, unlike today, even the least significant people in society took a great risk if they threw off the weight of tradition and decided to become his disciples.

And what of the Romans? The Greek-influenced Roman world presented an opposite threat: pagan and polytheistic, greedy and powerful, the Romans wanted no trouble. They cared not at all about this god or that, as long as their Caesar's divinity and authority was not challenged. From their point of view, Christianity was only one new expression of the strange Jewish religion. So be it, a god is a god and crazy Jewish prophets were a dime a dozen in the hills of Judea. Christianity was, as Judaism was, a pesky bug on the skin of a giant.

We know a few Roman citizens came to believe in Jesus while he was alive, but it was under the brilliant leadership of the apostle Paul, himself a Roman citizen, and other first-century Christians who traveled throughout the Roman world that the gospel rapidly spread. E. M. Blaiklock describes the world these Christians faced:

"The Christian faith came to a world hungry, and insecure and un-satisfied, to a morally disintegrating society, and to utter religious confusion."[4] Great wisdom was required to penetrate that society with the gospel.

*Back to the present.* Did any of that sound familiar? Some Christians today, like some ancient Jews, are burdened with some nonessential traditions while at the same time are quite unfamiliar with Jesus himself. Some, like the Romans, are ready to say "whatever"—whatever you believe is fine, as long as your truth doesn't disturb my truth. In the United States the audience includes a small number of people who genuinely embrace other religions.[5] They are like the devout Romans and Greeks whom Jesus faced. Finally, an even smaller number (8 percent) of the United States population strongly doubt the existence of God or, at least, have no faith in a living God. Now how are we to reach all of these people?

Clearly, filled with "treasures of wisdom and knowledge" (Col 2:3), Jesus knew what he was doing when he told his disciples he would teach them to fish for people. While the methods for evangelism change with culture and circumstance, the message remains unchanged. The model Jesus chose remains viable.

Wisdom as a characteristic of evangelism can be summed up in two words: *practice* and *patience.* It is estimated that today it takes about four years of evangelistic work before an unbeliever comes to faith.[6] This is no small matter for those of us who are easily frustrated by stoplights that hold up our progress for two minutes or by computers that fail to respond by nanoseconds. Learning to evangelize, like learning to fish, is a matter of experience. It's a never-ending process of watching, waiting, witnessing and plainly enjoying the people God so dearly loves. It's the practice of presenting truth, and it's surely a certain amount of failing to do it well. It's a matter of praying backward and forward. I look back at my attempts at evangelism, both successful and unsuccessful, and ask God to show me what I need to learn from those experiences. Then I look forward to new opportunities, praying for the Lord's leading.

I make time to be quiet and alone, and I ask God to lead me through the next experience.

## A STRANGER'S STORY

God always prepares us for what he invites us to do. The story I am about to tell you was prefaced by a day of renewal.

I was bone weary from working on a difficult project that was not going well. So I carved out of my schedule a one-day vacation, a day of doing things I love to do. On this particular day I went to a couple of my favorite art galleries in Los Angeles: I caught an exhibit at the Los Angeles County Museum. Later I went to a fine-arts theater to see the documentary *La Ciudad*, about Mexican immigrants living in Manhattan. After this brilliant film I left the theater with my mind and emotions reeling. Reading the review of the film had not prepared me for its emotional impact. It was now evening and I was hungry and tired, although rejuvenated, and more than ready to go home.

When I got in my car, I found I was very nearly out of gas. My heart sank as I drove down the street. A cold November wind whipped against the car, and my light daytime clothing proved no match for it. With great relief I soon saw a gas station on my left. I quickly cut across four lanes of heavy traffic on Wilshire Boulevard and pulled up to a pump. To my annoyance, I discovered I had to pay inside the station. I pushed open my car door, locked it behind me, ducked my head against the whipping wind and ran toward the building. I was already close to losing all the calm the day had brought when I nearly collided with an old green Oldsmobile sedan parked where no car should be parked—directly blocking access to the door. At that point I was not feeling calm. At that point all I could do was grumble.

Getting inside didn't help. The customer space was grungy and obviously neglected. My cursory glance confirmed that the one woman ahead of me in line matched the place perfectly. Her badly bleached hair hung limply and showed signs of a desperately needed root job. She asked the clerk for a brand of cigarettes that the two attendants couldn't find. *Great,* I thought. *I'm going to be stuck in this dirty, ugly space for at least ten minutes.* That the door was open and wind was blowing in didn't help one bit. In this assault on my well-sculpted day, the only thing being fueled was my frustration.

Then I noticed what else the woman in front of me was purchasing. In her rough and unkempt hands she held a power drink, an energy bar and a large bottle of soda. I suspected this was her dinner. She was sighing, and it registered with me that she was tired and, apparently, felt as hurried as I felt. Just as this awareness struck, I heard a horn honking and I noticed that in the Oldsmobile there was a little girl, impatient for her mother. Her mom then muttered through clenched teeth, "If she does that again, I'll kill her."

My first response was to judge her, to construct a little homily in my own mind on the perils of violence in the home when, just as suddenly, my thoughts shifted to her human plight. Clearly this woman had had enough. Before I could think about it —and if I had, surely I would have talked myself out of it—I put my hand on her arm. She turned quickly to face me. "Do you need me to pray for you?" I asked with tenderness that I knew came from God.

I had the feeling from her response that Jesus was in that convenience store, calling me to come from the theater two blocks away. He used my empty gas tank as the invitation.

Tears gushed from her eyes as she responded. "Yes, I do," she said. "I've spent the whole day at the hospital where my father is dying. My husband died before our baby was born. My mother died two years ago. It seems like everyone I love is leaving me. I need you to pray for me."

With neither of us shutting our eyes—and with the two Arab attendants intently listening and watching—I prayed for a few minutes for her and for her father. I watched as God lifted her anxiety. The room was transformed from grungy to glorious. When I was finished praying, I assured her that God loved her and would be with her. Then I asked her if she had a church in Los Angeles. "No, I don't, but I should," she said in a way that made me think she had thought about church long before this moment. I was able to tell her about a wonderful church in the area. I encouraged her to go and find a spiritual support system for the grief she was feeling.

With compassion I then reminded her, "There's one person who hasn't left you and that's your little girl, waiting for you in the car." Then I saw how effective God's wisdom is. "Yes!" she responded with her first smile. "I don't know what I would do without her. She's been with me in the hospital all day, and I know that she's upset and tired."

I dared not go further. Her daughter was bouncing from seat to seat and window to window. She was as spent as her mother. For days I carried a burden for this woman. I prayed fervently. I felt as though I was "mending nets," repairing her misconceptions of God and preparing her for further evangelism.

Someday this woman may turn to a church for help. She may even come to your church. She will be looking for someone "full of mercy and good fruit" (Jas 3:17). She will be looking for evidence of wisdom. How might you respond?

## ENGAGE IN BECOMING WISE

1. What struck you as important in this chapter?

2. What in the image of evangelism as "fishing for people" appeals to you? What in this image presents you with the greatest challenge?

3. Read James 3:13, 17.

   a. Briefly state what you think worldly wisdom is.

   b. Explain how God's wisdom differs from worldly wisdom.

   c. What challenges does a Christian today have in developing godly wisdom?

d. Think of an unbeliever who would benefit from your application of Christian wisdom as shown in this text. What would you need to do to bring God's wisdom to them?

e. Prayerfully set about applying God's wisdom in this situation. Take note of your challenges and your attitudes, as well as your friend's response, as you follow through.

# 7
# PATIENT

## THE ANATOMY OF PERSUASION

*On every level of life from housework to heights of prayer,*
*in all judgment and all efforts to get things done,*
*hurry and impatience are sure marks of an amateur.*

EVELYN UNDERHILL

*The wind blows wherever it pleases. You hear its sound,*
*but you cannot tell where it comes from or where it is going.*
*So it is with everyone born of the Spirit.*

JOHN 3:8

**WE KNOW THAT** patience is the ability to endure. In evangelism it involves enduring through
the process of persuading our unbelieving friends
to follow Jesus as King with their thoughts, emotions and behaviors.

In our quest to follow Jesus as he seeks and saves the lost through us (Lk 19:10), our mission will be incomplete or unsuccessful unless we have a working understanding of persuasion and the patience to see it through. Most traditional approaches to evangelism use a partial approach, focusing on the mental component of salvation.

Evangelism involves the whole person: the mind that thinks, the heart that feels, the body that acts.

Our minds must be convinced that Jesus is God, that we are sinful, that Jesus died on the cross to make salvation possible for us, and that through his resurrection we have been liberated to live (with the help of the Holy Spirit) a life that is better than any life we would have without him.

Emotionally we must feel that following Jesus is right and good for us. We must believe Jesus with our hearts. But here's the rub—some of our own wants aren't good. Because emotions can be strong, we often go with them, regardless of what our minds know. The mind is often an unwanted presence from the viewpoint of sinful passions and feeling. Evangelism that bypasses emotions, therefore, will likely fail.

Finally, what good is it to believe in something if our behavior doesn't match our belief? Consider smoking. Many people who smoke *believe* smoking is dangerous, but they do not quit. Belief is only admirable if it is powerful enough to affect change. Salvation prompts changed behavior. Knowing how Jesus acted, what he did in various situations, invites us to change our own behavior. We become like him through change thorough enough, fundamental enough, to require a lifetime.

A challenging component of evangelism is that the minds, emotions and behaviors of at least two people are at work: the Christian who prayerfully persuades and the nonbeliever whose mind, emotions and behaviors are being challenged. Any Christian who approaches an unbeliever must be fully aware of his or her own personal imperfections—imperfections that our emotionally threatened nonbelieving friends are often willing to point out. ("Well, *you* aren't perfect!") We must live transparently enough that this objection is ludicrous. Persuasion is most effective when it is obvious to others that our own beliefs, attitudes and behaviors are honestly open to a God who invites change. We are only qualified to encourage in others what is observable in our own lives. When a newly converted person happily follows Jesus as King, it is because the whole person was turned around. The mind, emotions and behaviors all responded.

## PATIENCE WITH THE RELUCTANT OR SHY INQUIRER

Just as there are Christians who are reluctant or shy about sharing their faith, there are many unbelievers who are also reticent when it comes to inquiring about Jesus. For reasons as various as the people who hold them, they are hesitant to admit that Jesus might matter. Christians should pray for the wind of God's Spirit to move on them, and we should patiently wait for the evidence of their becoming spiritually open. God is gently persuading them to turn to Jesus. If we understand this, it will be easier for us to be patient. In persuasive evangelism, hurriedness and impatience are the marks of an amateur or at least a sign that we are meddling with God's intentions.

The Spirit blew on Nicodemus. John tells us that he was so influenced by Jesus that he sought a private conversation with him *at night!* Why did he first approach Jesus when it was dark? It is quite possible that he was afraid of being seen talking to Jesus. After all, as a Pharisee, Nicodemus had his reputation to protect. Or perhaps he was shy. But the Spirit was compelling enough for him to knock on Jesus' door. The apostle John places this encounter in the first year of Jesus' ministry. The richness of the dialogue suggests to some theologians that Jesus spent a long night, probably until the next morning, speaking to Nicodemus profound truths that set him apart from all religious teachers. Then Nicodemus vanishes and we have no record that the two ever talked again. But that isn't the end of the story.

After two years have passed Nicodemus surfaces again. John 7 begins by saying the Judean religious leaders were looking for an opportunity to kill Jesus. Later in the chapter we find Nicodemus meeting with the chief priests and Pharisees of Jerusalem who were greatly disturbed by the growing number of people following Jesus. They resolved to quell this group by sending temple priests to arrest Jesus, but the priests returned empty handed, saying, "Never has anyone spoken like this!" (Jn 7:46 NRSV).

In that heated meeting Nicodemus challenged his colleagues to give Jesus a hearing (Jn 7:50-52). While he was not openly declaring himself a disciple, he was courageously speaking up for Jesus. It would be my guess that for many months he pondered his conversation with Jesus. No doubt he stayed abreast of Jesus' ministry during this time and, whether or not he was ready to commit himself, he couldn't discount him.

We see further spiritual development in Nicodemus after Jesus' death. Along with Joseph of Arimathea, he claimed the body of the crucified Jesus and saw to the proper preparation for his burial (Jn 19:38-40). To take so great a social and religious risk without having first thoroughly aligned himself with Jesus seems unlikely. Still, we can't be sure what he had decided.

Clearly not even Jesus expected every conversion to occur instantaneously. But in light of this story, we learn that sometimes he was patiently working behind the scenes through a process of persuasion. Jesus devoted time to persuading Nicodemus that he was true, credible, essential, commendable and worthy. And we can assume that disciples like Joseph of Arimathea were being used in God's unhurried, persuasive work with Nicodemus.

## THE DIVINE KIND OF PERSUASION

I was talking recently with a very successful salesman about persuasion, and he told me that he learned most of what he knows during college, when he was selling pots and pans. "If a salesman does his job with integrity, thoroughness and enthusiasm, there comes a point when the buyer persuades himself. The salesperson can leave the room and return to collect money for the sale."

I think we see that truth in the story of Zacchaeus, a man so ready to be a disciple of Jesus that he appears to have been instantaneously converted. It even looks like he persuaded himself to become a disciple. Nevertheless, we must be cautious before drawing that conclusion. The prophet Jeremiah explains we have perverse and devious hearts (Jer 17:9). It's highly unlikely that a shrewd man like Zacchaeus woke up one morning deciding to give his life to Jesus. It's more reasonable and likely to think of God's Spirit patiently preparing Zacchaeus's soul for a long time before he encountered Jesus. Here we see a demonstration of divine patience and divine persuasion.

Zacchaeus's personality is altogether different from Nicodemus's. He appears bold, headstrong and inwardly desperate. Nicodemus was led to Jesus by his mind. Zacchaeus was led to Jesus by his heart. If there are fan clubs in heaven, I'll be the first in line to sign up for Zacchaeus's. Something about him always reminds me that God's marvelous sense of humor is laced with contagious grace. When we meet Zacchaeus in Scripture he's hanging on to the branch of a sycamore tree. No doubt he is perspiring from having run to get ahead of the crowd following Jesus. Zacchaeus was cunning and determined. He knew Jesus was entering Jericho and, because he was short, he hustled, climbed a sycamore tree, oblivious to the opinion of the crowd or the likely damage to his fine clothes.

Here's what we know. For some reason he chose an occupation guaranteed to gain him the disapproval of all other Jews. He was a chief tax collector, taxing his own people for Rome and, in the process, taxing the tax for his own comfortable income. Scratch friendships off the list of what he had. Add inappropriate emotions and behaviors. He was obviously materialistic enough to abandon his national allegiances in order to get rich. I suspect he was jaded by religion, having seen the bankruptcy of legalism from his peers and the folly of chasing after Roman gods. Nonetheless, the tree-climbing episode revealed his spiritual appetite. He knew enough about the uniqueness of Jesus to throw down propriety and shimmy up the tree in the hopes of seeing and hearing something that would meet his needs.

Enter Jesus, full of gracious enthusiasm. He stopped in front of the tree and proclaimed in a voice loud enough to rise above any crowd noise, "Zacchaeus, come down immediately. I must stay at your house today" (Lk 19:5). Who could have expected that! Jesus called him by name and invited, no, demanded relationship. Zacchaeus immediately understood that he was neither scorned nor rejected but unconditionally accepted. He "came down at once and welcomed him gladly" (Lk 19:6). His encounter with Jesus resulted in a change of heart and behavior. Zacchaeus may have still been off the ground when he began his response.

> "Look, Lord! Here and now I give half of my possessions to the poor, and if I have cheated anybody out of anything, I will pay back four times the amount."
>
> Jesus said to him, "Today salvation has come to this house, because this man, too, is a son of Abraham. For the Son of Man came to seek and to save what was lost." (Lk 19:8-10)

It takes less than two minutes to read this story in the Gospel of Luke, yet we can imagine that it took patience on God's part to prepare Zacchaeus for that moment. Make no mistake about it, God was seeking and Jesus was there when the time was right, when desperation sent a small man up a tree.

When I come face to face with this man Zacchaeus, I want to ask him, "Why? How? What? Why did a rich guy like you resort to climbing a tree? Wasn't there an easier way to hear Jesus? How did wealth lend to your spiritual hunger? Did something in the Jewish law dissatisfy you enough to make this odious affiliation with Rome? What did you hear about Jesus that prepared you to respond as you did? And what did it mean to you to have Jesus call out your name?"

The conversion of Zacchaeus is an ideal example of the divine persuasion we are considering. His mind accepted the authority of Jesus, his heart caused him to happily welcome him, and his behavior quickly revealed that he was committed to the teaching of Jesus. Is there any way to effectively evangelize other than to convince an unbeliever that Jesus is true, credible, essential, commendable and worthy?

We can also learn from this story what persuasion is not. Emory Griffin states a standard for evangelism that is evident in this story: "Any persuasive effort which restricts another's freedom to choose for or against Jesus Christ is wrong."[1] Jesus did not coerce or force Zacchaeus to convert, neither was Zacchaeus manipulated in any way. There's nothing devious in this encounter, no hint of deception that leads to buyer's remorse. We see Zacchaeus respond quickly because he was spiritually ready to be persuaded. Therefore it shouldn't surprise us to learn that those who are the most persuasive in evangelism are those who are the least manipulative. They know how to read people, and they depend on God to give them the information or the experience they need to help others take their next necessary step toward Jesus.

I have seen people shy away from becoming Christians because they weren't willing to change their behavior. I have watched people reject Christianity because they did not yet see it as intellectually sound, even though they wanted a faith like the one a Christian friend experienced and even though they approved of their friend's behavior. I have also seen people receive Christ when one of these areas wasn't yet in alignment. Care must then be taken in the church to persuade the new Christian of the importance of facing whatever prevents him or her from serving Jesus as King.

When I was a new Christian, I found a poster that was important enough to me to hang in my office. "You have not converted a man because you have silenced him." We must avoid the mistake of equating silence with success. We can silence someone with an oppressive or aggressive attitude: for example, blurting into a person's situation with "What you really need is Jesus." I'd like a new poster that reads, "You have not persuaded someone to become a Christian until that person chooses to follow Christ with mind, emotions and behaviors." That's success.

Persuasion requires a process that Griffin has simplified to these three stages: melt, mold and make hard.[2] This progression comes to my mind each time I visit our family's foundry. A foundry is a place where old metals are melted and poured into molds to make new products. Our particular foundry makes counterweights used to counterbalance the heavy loads carried by tractors, forklifts and cranes. Without counterweights the loads will flip heavy equipment as easily as an unintentional nudge flips the full tray of dishes held high by a busy waiter. Counterweights are made through the process of "melting, molding and making hard."

## MELTING

Scrap iron is placed in the cupola, foundry terminology for a furnace, where it is heated to the right consistency for pouring, 2400 degrees Fahrenheit. Iron is not all that resists having its shape changed. People resist change too. Yet there is no simple formula, such as "heat person to 2400 degrees and the person will be ready for a mold." Melting a person's resistance is not a formula, it is a commitment. It requires our watching carefully for signs of mental, emotional and behavioral readiness.

Gravel rolls around in the furnace with the iron to collect impurities in the scrap metal. Such impurities might include rust, coating material, oil or anything clinging to the scrap metal when it's dumped into the cupola. It's natural for old iron to have impurities, but if they aren't removed they create defects on the casting. Heat and gravel work together to remove the impurities.

What substitute does God use for gravel in the lives of seekers today? What is it that causes a person to become curious enough to be even slightly open to Jesus? We can't get standard answers to these questions, but we can safely assume that when God nudges us toward an unbeliever that person is either already inwardly disturbed or will become unsettled by our presence in a way that will begin preparing them for the gospel.

We can play a significant role in "melting" our unbelieving friends when we share our personal struggles with them. When their impurities come up, we can encourage them by pointing them to God and recalling how he's carried us through similar trials. We can be transparent about our own struggle with sin, honestly speaking of our failures and also of the times when by faith we overcome sin. We can stand in the furnace with them.

Honestly identifying with non-Christians in their struggle with sin is an important part of their melting process. "Sin is a lump," writes Kenneth Leech.[3] We're all in it together, and we will stay together in that lump throughout our earthly journey. But the purging of sin is also an ongoing event. Jesus died on the cross for sin—past, present and any possibility ahead. That's the good news of purifying heat.

## MOLDING

When melting iron reaches the right temperature it becomes white. At this stage the impurities are skimmed off the top and the liquid iron is poured into a ladle, similar to a large pitcher. The ladle is then connected to a hoist that carries it to the mold, which consists of a bowl and a lid held together by a clamp. Iron is poured through one hole and filled until it comes out a second hole, signaling that the mold is full. Filled, the mold stays undisturbed until the iron is thoroughly solidified.

During the molding process our spiritually open friends are watching us closely. Our actions, our attitudes and behaviors have great bearing on the shape of their response to faith. During this phase it's critical that they see credible Christians. They will be keeping a watchful eye on us, looking to see whether we maintain a consistent standard. Here are some things Griffin suggests we do:[4]

*Increase in credibility.* If someone asks a question you can't answer, say, "I need to think about this. I'll get back to you." Don't lose the respect of your audience by being sloppy with your information. Study your Bible, call your pastor, do whatever it takes to give an accurate, authoritative response. If the subject is outside your ability to answer, simply say that you don't know. Credible people neither try to lead people through unfamiliar territory nor give superficial answers to substantive questions.

*Find points of agreement with your friend.* This is the first principle of crosscultural communication. In evangelism you represent a Christian culture while your pre-Christian friend represents an entirely different one. Listen carefully. Your friends may verbally package what they think or feel in a manner different from how you would, but if you look for points of agreement, you will find them. See how you can build bridges instead of walls.

*Increase trustworthiness.* Spend time with those you wish to influence. Watch for signs that alert you that you have said enough. Deep trust requires your proximity and your loyalty. When you're spending time with your friend, watch your tongue. Speak the truth and consistently speak well of others. Let Jesus be the guest that listens to all you choose to say.

*Engage in the difficult task of self-disclosure.* When we share our innermost struggles and our greatest joys, others relax. We prove ourselves genuine. Masks slip off and pertinent dialogue replaces shallow conversation.

*Increase your dynamism.* Allow your excitement about who God is and what he's doing in your life to create a lilt in your voice. Let the wonder of what it means to be saved rise from your heart and into your conversation. There's nothing more unconvincing than a predictable, packaged testimony. Enthusiasm is contagious; it is the perfect word for this stage. We are the mold that is enthused, filled with God, and sharing that it is exciting.

## MAKING HARD

Imagine what would happen if a counterweight was removed from the mold prematurely, before it was made hard. Since molds prepare iron for specific purposes, its inability to hold its shape makes it unfit for use. The initial time, energy and risk involved in melting and pouring would be for nothing. Foundry workers dare not be impatient. Like it or not, impatient or not, they succeed because they honor the time required for melted metal inside the mold to harden, that is, to be tempered to retain its proper shape. When that time has expired, the product is tested for readiness by being so violently shaken that the mold falls off. Here is the good news: no amount of shaking is going to redefine this product. It is ready for use.

I wish it really were that easy to deal with people! Hardening a person's resolve to serve Jesus Christ as King depends on many more variables. But the process is similar to that of making counterweights —risk, time, experience, testing and patience.

Endurance lies at the heart of what it means to be patient, but endurance is something few of us greet with enthusiasm. I've endured and, more honestly, suffered the discomfort of having a nonbeliever confront me with my un-Christian behavior. I've agonized over my mistakes of pushing people too hard or too fast. I've cried over missed opportunities that happened before I came to understand that a person's thoughts, feelings and behaviors must all be addressed in evangelism. It is as we experience and review our failures, as we learn the difficult work of being self-reflective, that we learn to read people like fishermen learn to read the water.

## WHEN PATIENCE TURNS PERSONAL

Patience seems to be a quality that many of us want to have. But most of us balk at the actual process of learning to be patient. I don't recommend having a brain aneurysm as a good lesson, but that is what taught me the deepest lessons about patience. The grueling reality of being a hospital patient for a month only to be released into a slow-moving recovery taught me a great deal.

My lesson began while holding a stretch in a fitness class. The next thing I knew, fifteen women were standing over me, their faces etched with concern. I don't remember the helicopter ride to the UCLA Medical Center. I don't remember any of my three weeks' stay there except the moans coming from fellow patients in the intensive-care unit.

Once I was at the rehabilitation facility, I started the arduous process of regaining my abilities through physical, speech and occupational therapies. I couldn't write, type or even walk straight. My mind had to be retrained in "divergent thinking." When I came home, all my time was organized around getting the proper rest and being taken to my various therapy appointments; driving was out of the question.

Going from an active lifestyle to that of an invalid was extremely difficult for me until God spoke to me during a time of prayer when I had poured out my complaints. "This aneurysm isn't about you, Chris, it's about me."

Suddenly I realized that I hadn't really suffered great pain, at least none that I remembered. There were things about my life that would never be the same, but whose life remains unchanged? I was fortunate to be alive at all. Very few people survive the assault my brain experienced or the eight hours of surgery that followed. I work hard at recovery and to do it, I have simply had to learn to be patient with myself.

God's words to me fit well into the model for evangelism. "Evangelism is not about you, Chris, it's about me."

God will bring people to us that we, at first, don't think we are qualified to evangelize. Perhaps we feel too busy. Or maybe they are more talented, too far from God, too educated or even not educated enough. God puts particular people in our path for their sake and for ours. We learn patience with them as we learn how to persuade their minds, hearts and behaviors to come to Jesus Christ and serve him as King.

We can learn so much from Paul, the first evangelist and missionary to the Gentiles. He traveled throughout a world replete with dangers, disease and a pantheon of oppressive gods. Here's how he described his means of persuasion and the audience he addressed:

Therefore, since through God's mercy we have this ministry, we do not lose heart. Rather, we have renounced secret and shameful ways; we do not use deception, nor do we distort the word of God. On the contrary, by setting forth the truth plainly we commend ourselves to every man's conscience in the sight of God. And even if our gospel is veiled, it is veiled to those who are perishing. The god of this age has blinded the minds of unbelievers, so that they cannot see the light of the gospel of the glory of Christ, who is the image of God. For we do not preach ourselves, but Jesus Christ as Lord, and ourselves as your servants for Jesus' sake. For God, who said, "Let light shine out of darkness," made his light shine in our hearts to give us the light of the knowledge of the glory of God in the face of Christ. (2 Cor 4:1-6)

It is important to take note of the information Paul gives us here because it applies to how we must evangelize. Mercy was his motivation for committing to evangelism. Yes, it was a seemingly impossible task for Paul, but he was compelled because he saw his audience as spiritually dying patients and himself as being sent by God to them, dispensing the Master's remedy. Since evangelism wasn't about him as much as it was about God, he trusted God for the heart and stamina to continue on.

Nothing in his persuasion strategy was devious. He refused to manipulate his audience. The power of his testimony came from a life consistent with the true words he taught. This is a crucial observation because his enemy, Satan, always is devious; he is the "the father of lies" (Jn 8:44). His strategy is to keep people in spiritual darkness. When we evangelize, we offer God's truth to expose Satan's charade. But Christians can only share the light that they carry. Nothing pierces the veil more powerfully than our own fresh experience with God. So it seems reasonable that Satan will do everything he can to dull our experience of God and to disturb our quiet time with him, the place where God wants to speak clearly to us.

Personally I don't know how to respond to Paul's powerful words except by attempting to apply them one day at a time, one person at a time. It's the only way I can do the job. Daily, in order to maintain my focus on God, I need to seek fresh guidance through reading Scripture and prayer. For it is God who "made his light shine in our hearts to give us the light of the knowledge of the glory of God in the face of Christ." Every day, I must "put on mercy" (another spiritual gift I don't possess and another role I am to assume), and every day I must look for the opportunities God gives me to practice it. In every situation I must patiently live out God's character in both word and deed. Satan will do all he can to oppose me but, every day, all day, God's strength is sufficient for me to overcome obstacles.

## KIM'S STORY

Perhaps the most challenging person I've ever worked to persuade is Kim. In fact, the task was so difficult I could only face it by thinking, *one day, one incident at a time.* Kim stands smack in the middle of her life. At forty she's the logical product of her secular Jewish upbringing and culture. She grew up in a wealthy family, dysfunctional to the core. Her father, largely uninvolved with her in childhood, has been married three times, as has her mother. The second of Kim's stepfathers was the worst. He brought three quarrelsome sons to this marriage and was partial to them throughout Kim's years growing up. He was apathetic and sometimes mean to Kim and her two sisters.

Now the sisters are middle-aged women captured by a completely secular mindset. They are by most standards rich, and they manage to push materialism to an absurdly high level. Any social behavior short of crime is acceptable to them, from adultery to visiting fortune-tellers. They live a frantic life, gathering experiences to entertain themselves or to diffuse the pain of childhood and the present doubts of validity. Kim has always felt unsettled in her family, different from her relatives in some of her values yet needing their approval. Sometimes, mainly for acceptance and because she hasn't been taught differently, she dips back into their motto: "It doesn't really matter what you do, as long as you're happy."

Interestingly, Kim has always believed God exists. She married a Christian and sporadically attended church with him. She was unwilling to become a Christian because she thought she had no need of salvation. The marriage floundered and became a bitter disappointment to her. So in trying to find what made her happy, she left her husband and moved with their three children to a house nearby. She acted out her anger in the sinful ways she'd learned from her family. After a few months consequences of her choices began to hit. Her mind was melted enough to think the time was right for salvation.

And so with her mind, she became a Christian. It was her husband's privilege to pray with her to receive Christ. The immediate result was threefold. First, she had inner peace. Second, she began praying. Third, the Bible became interesting to her. By many definitions we could say that Kim had been evangelized.

However, our definition of evangelism includes serving Jesus as King. Kim had emotional and behavioral issues that needed to be addressed if they were going to be changed. At the moment of her conversion she knew that she needed the forgiveness that only Jesus made available, but she knew little else about how her life would be affected. She was unaware that following him meant dealing with personal issues of mind, emotions and behaviors.

For one thing, Kim remained angry with her husband. Following the pattern of women in her family, she sought a divorce. She continued in sinful habits that exacerbated the tension between her and her spouse, and they both avoided some of the issues that lent to their family schism.

It was at this point that I began spiritual work with Kim. Although we had known each other casually for several years, we had never talked about Christian formation. She respected me enough to submit herself to the rigors involved in spiritual growth. One of the first things we did was travel to her mother's city to spend the day with her. We went to a museum and we went out to lunch at her mother's posh country club. Kim drove me past her grandparents' lavish house in one of the most exclusive areas of the city. Kim remembers their love for her as being the most heartwarming part of her childhood. In that same neighborhood, Kim drove me past the homes of her best childhood friends, and I noticed how lovingly she spoke of them. Today Kim is still in touch with many of them, and I began to understand why her unbelieving friends in her present community are so important to her.

Kim also pointed out the places where she played as a child, some of which are now occupied by skyscrapers. I noticed sadness in her voice as she described changes to me. It seemed as though part of Kim wanted to be back in that time, removed from the adult problems she had to face every day. I began to form a more complete picture of her past, and I acquired a deeper appreciation of the hurdles she would have to clear if she were to serve Jesus as King. Insight into how she thinks, feels and acts proved invaluable to me as I worked to encourage her growth.

For some people, old habits seem to evaporate when that person receives Christ; but for others, their habits die a hard, painful death. This is the case with Kim. Thus far, we have suffered a lot together. The lines between the melting and molding process can't be as clearly identified as they are at a foundry. What is patently clear is the absolute need for patience in our relationship. Kim needs patience in the work of restructuring her life that salvation requires. In her mind she wants to trust Jesus to change her. In her heart she's terrified that somehow God will let her down, just as her parents have done. In the meantime, her life doesn't get easier. The habits and consequences of living forty years without God have a terribly firm grip on her. She has to be patient with me because I am a reminder to her of needed change. Yes, her conversion was miraculous, but the changes are not instantaneous.

That's why Kim needs a trusted Christian friend to be patient with her in this process. I can do it through the power of the Holy Spirit, but usually only one day at a time. On a good day I can be patient with Kim because I can see how patient God is with me. On other days the unfinished parts in me want to pull off to the sidelines and quit. Then the Spirit reminds me that patience is the ability to endure

through the process of persuading our unbelieving friends to follow
Jesus as King with their thoughts, emotions and behaviors. My
thoughts, emotions and behaviors must be continually recommitted
to Jesus, the One who persuades me to follow him.

## ENGAGE IN BECOMING PATIENT

1. What did you find useful in this chapter?

2. Which part of persuading—thoughts, emotions or behaviors—is
   most natural for you? Which part is hardest? Give reasons for
   your answers.

3. How do you suggest you turn your weakness into an area of
   strength?

4. Read the story in Luke 15:11-24.

   a. How does the father demonstrate patience?

   b. How can we tell that the young son was fully persuaded in his
      mind, emotions, and behavior that he should go back to his fa-
      ther's house?

   c. What application for persuasive evangelism do you find in this
      story?

# 8

# EMPATHETIC

## CULTIVATING A LISTENING EAR
## AND AN ENCOURAGING TONGUE

*As Jesus and his disciples were on their way,*
*he came to a village where a woman named Martha*
*opened her home to him. She had a sister called Mary, who sat*
*at the Lord's feet listening to what he said.*
*But Martha was distracted by all the preparations*
*that had to be made. She came to him and asked,*
*"Lord, don't you care that my sister has left me to do the work by myself?*
*Tell her to help me!"*

*"Martha, Martha," the Lord answered, "you are worried and upset*
*about many things, but only one thing is needed.*
*Mary has chosen what is better,*
*and it will not be taken away from her."*

LUKE 10:38-42

EMPATHY is the capacity to enter into another's
ideas feelings and desires, first in listening and
then in offering an appropriate response. The most
effective evangelists learn to listen before speaking, and in so doing they encourage their non-
Christian friends.

Most of us have heard the story in Luke's Gospel about Jesus' visit to Mary and Martha's home. We who are "doers" easily relate to Martha.

Mary had cultivated a listening ear, one bent toward Jesus. She gave him her full attention. When Mary was criticized by her sister for being inconsiderate and neglectful, Jesus responded with empathy, entering her feelings and offering genuine encouragement. Mary, too, was demonstrating empathy in the way she listened to Jesus. Jesus declared Mary's behavior to be right and gently corrected her critical sister.

Imagine for a moment being accused of doing something you absolutely did not do. Not only did you not do what it looked like you were doing, but the thought had never even entered your mind! It's more than possible that you've actually experienced such a situation, or surely you will some day. I don't think Mary thought, *I won't help. I'll sit right here and pretend to be preoccupied with Jesus' teaching.* I think she was utterly captivated. She was avid, not avoiding.

I am forever indebted to the teacher who, early in my Christian journey, shared a piece of wisdom that has shaped the way I approach life. He said there are only two things in life that will last forever: Scripture and human beings. Realizing this has helped me set my priorities to evangelize. How simple it is to say, "I must devote my attention to these two eternal priorities." How difficult it is to do it. Nonetheless, such focus is foundational to evangelism.

Interestingly, both Scripture and people must be approached with a listening heart. Only after one truly hears can one properly respond. Isn't it often the opposite with us concerning these two vital things? We approach Scripture with a problem or a desire and we seek to find the answer we want. We approach our non-Christian friends with a "solution" before we ever bother to hear their problem.

We have much to learn, but our lifestyle discourages listening as the means of learning. Little in our culture encourages listening for long. We are accustomed to hearing in spurts: horns, lids clanging, quick calls, TV and radio commercials and programming that deliberately feed us sound "bites." Amidst the frantic pace of our technological world, we have learned to pay rapt attention only to things that startle us—pain, gossip, a failing relationship or a financial crisis. For many of us eternal priorities are hardly noticeable; they are far, far down the long list of urgent things to do or hear.

## Working Up a Relational Sweat

Listening requires work. M. Scott Peck describes his experience with it:

> Not very long ago I attended a lecture by a famous man on an aspect of the relationship between psychology and religion in which I have long been interested. Because of my interest I had a certain amount of expertise in the subject and immediately recognized the lecturer to be a great sage indeed. I also sensed love in the tremendous effort that he was exerting to communicate . . . highly abstract concepts that were difficult for us . . . to comprehend. I . . . listened to him with . . . intentness. . . . Throughout the hour and a half he talked sweat was literally dripping down my face in the air-conditioned auditorium. By the time he was finished I had a throbbing headache, the muscles in my neck were rigid from my effort at concentration, and I felt completely drained and exhausted, . . . amazed by the large number of brilliant insights he had given me.[1]

Peck goes on to describe his experience of listening to individuals who attended the lecture.

> Generally they were disappointed. Knowing his reputation, they had expected more. They found him hard to follow and his talk confusing. He was not as competent a speaker as they had hoped to hear. One woman proclaimed to nods of agreement, "He really didn't tell us anything."

What accounts for the difference in the audience's perceptions? How they listened. Listening involves more than hearing. Listening pays attention to details: tone of voice, repetition of words, sighs, silence, eagerness, hesitation, awkwardness and tears. It requires effort, as Peck realized. Too few people bother to exert themselves as he did. Yet how can we hope to have significant dialogue with our unbelieving friends if we aren't entering into their ideas, feelings and desires by first really listening to them?

Evangelism is impossible apart from listening. Evangelism begins with listening to God, with concentration that causes us to sweat our way to new levels of thinking. He leads us to the people who need his salvation. The part he calls us to may surprise us. Maybe we will meet a particular non-Christian who holds a sour opinion of God's people and at the moment needs nothing more than to be intrigued by seeing joy in one who follows Jesus. Our task may be to witness or to pray with them to receive Christ. How much and how far are usually what we don't know as we follow God's leading. What we do know is that we must listen before we dare speak about Jesus. Otherwise we cannot respond with necessary empathy. We must remember that our words, however true they may be, fall flat without this prerequisite. It's the act of listening that prompts us to weep for our friends in pain and celebrate with those who have cause for celebration; it enables us to join with God and, as Morris West said, "embrace the world like a lover."[2] It enables us to join with God in truly hearing the ones he brings to us. We join with Mary of Bethany in choosing "the better part" and with psychiatrist Peck in listening so intently that we too work up a relational sweat.

## THE FULLNESS OF SALVATION

What comes to your mind when you hear the word *salvation*? Depending on what area of the country you're living in, the company you keep and your history of receiving Christian teaching, this word may have different connotations. For many churches I've visited and in conversations I've listened to, *salvation* means the initial act of praying to receive Jesus and insuring a place in heaven. This view fits, but it is severely truncated: we lack the vital understanding that God helps us every day with whatever we need to bring his kingdom to our part of this earth.

For many others, the term *salvation* is plainly offensive. To quote a lovely, sincere woman, "I'm a good person. I was born in America and this means that I'm a Christian. I don't need salvation!" To some, the concept of salvation is outdated, something old relatives spoke of.

Since the true meaning of this word is pivotal to Christian faith, isn't it important that we understand how people hear it? How do we offer the fullness of salvation today, and just what are we offering? We must begin by moving beyond the notion that salvation is only that critical moment when spiritual life begins. I believe that moment is indeed critical. I vividly remember thirty-one years ago when I asked God to come into my life. I can recall where I was standing, what I said and my experience of receiving an inner tranquility as powerful as the silence of guns after a long war. In the days that followed, my mind was filled with thoughts about God and Jesus. It remains so today. It is important to me that I am applying Scripture to my life. Consequently, my salvation today has expanded and deepened far beyond what happened that first moment I received Christ. The fullness of salvation is the ongoing richness of the dynamic life that I receive from God to live each day with its attending rewards and challenges. I am convinced God intends each of his children to experience salvation's fullness in whatever challenges the present moment presents.

One definition of salvation has to do with rescue from destruction.[3] This may apply to something as overt as a physical threat or as subtle as the undeserved shame that inevitably results from being unloved. In its fullness, salvation also expands to mean "restored to health," whether that is an obvious physical healing or a discreet act of healing unhealthy attitudes. Salvation also means "to be made whole again," restored to live according to God's image and likeness. Being healed as part of salvation can be instantaneous or ongoing.

In Romans 7:7—8:11, Paul describes how the fullness of salvation is received in process. We can become increasingly filled with the Holy Spirit and transformed into the likeness of Jesus Christ. Without Jesus in our lives, we are spiritually dead; we are cut off from the personal presence of God. However, with him, though we are "saved" instantly at the time we receive him, the fullness of our salvation continues to grow throughout our life, and we are made more and more whole. That is the good news.

The bad news is that even we Christians can avoid this wholeness or fullness that God makes available through Christ. We can choose to be surely saved but not daily saved—like a building made of only one wall. We always are free to turn away from opportunities God puts before us, refusing the chance to increase our mental and emotional knowledge of Jesus and ourselves. This, of course, affects how we live out our Christian faith and certainly how or whether we evangelize.

Our daily experience with the multifaceted aspects of salvation provides the material we need for sharing Christ. For example, when an unbeliever is considering a decision that surely will produce negative consequences, we can humbly share a time when we were similarly tempted and how God met us and led us differently. When someone's confidence is placed in us and our confidence is in Jesus, we are able to influence change. The point is this: our ongoing experience with salvation is more than the hope of heaven; it is also a bridge that connects us to our non-Christian friends.

I have a friend who, when she was a teenager, would occasionally come home from school to find that her mother had lavishly shopped for her. Skirts, sweaters, dresses and shoes would be scattered over her bed, and she was allowed to choose those items she wanted to keep. Those experiences told her that someone cared. Someone obviously knew what she liked, even loved. Someone took time for her. Someone offered a no-strings-attached gift. Salvation is like that. It is the most perfect gift God could ever have given us. He knows what we need and what we love. He lays it out for us. We are free to choose it, and we are meant to wear it happily. In wearing it, we remember that God is alive to us and that we can count on his creative care.

Salvation, experienced daily, has a cumulative effect over the years. My knowledge, my store, of God's salvation today is much more substantive than it was the first day God's Spirit set up residence in me. This gift is what we have the privilege of sharing, even to the ends of the earth (Acts 1:8).

## PARTNERING WITH GOD IN EVANGELISM

There are some things only God can do. We are not partners in the work of redemption (Col 1:13-14). We were nowhere around when creation was a notion, and we dare not weigh in on the glory of God. But aspects of our being have been created in his likeness. And he partners with us as we think, create, love and make decisions. In our calling to evangelism we move in harmony with his Spirit in order to deliver God's good news to our world. It resembles much of what Jesus did when he took on flesh and lived among us, only he, being God, was able to participate in redemption (Jn 5:17, 19).

When the founder of Bible Study Fellowship, A. Wetherell Johnson, invited me to the leader training, I caught a glimpse of what it meant to be a full but not equal partner. I knew that I was not assuming responsibilities equal to hers, that I was thoroughly untrained to teach, and that her schedule was far more demanding and complex than my own. Yet when we discussed the date for my training, she treated me as a full partner in the ministry she had founded by offering me options from which to choose. She treated me with great respect and, by her example, laid the foundation of how I was to treat the leaders who partnered with me in our local Bible Study Fellowship class. Ms. Johnson trusted me. I still remember the joy I felt when I decided to partner with her in ministry, even though it was a nonsalaried position that required many hours of hard work each week.

To partner with God in evangelism is much the same. He invites us into a position of training and trust. He invites us to listen to his instructions concerning the people with whom we interact. He calls us to pay attention to the opportunities he makes available.

In my experience, evangelism is more about listening to God than talking to people, more about listening to others than speaking. This listening means paying attention to detail: tone of voice, repetition of words, sighs, silence, eagerness, hesitation, awkwardness, tears. Listening requires the sweat of concentration. It means that we respond appropriately to signals from another, that our responses prove beneficial to that person at that unique moment—a moment that will never be repeated. "Do not let any unwholesome talk come out of your mouths, but only what is helpful for building others up according to their needs, that it may benefit those who listen" (Eph 4:29). When we give others this kind of attention, our partnership with God becomes *visible* to them, and they are drawn to it. The words we speak after concerned and compassionate listening yield a spiritual power that graciously persuades people to earnestly desire a relationship with the One who loved them before the world was formed. He is Immanuel, God with them, when they weep and when they celebrate.

## ROXANA'S STORY

I am grateful that I listened to God the day I met Roxana.

I needed clothes for a special event and decided to go to a store that offers a personal shopper. As I drove there, I recognized that I was too busy, too hurried, too focused on my task to think that God may have some work for us to do together. So on my way I prayed for my relationship with the personal shopper and for speed in moving through what I hoped would not be an ordeal.

Everything went together smoothly. My selections were pleasantly and swiftly completed, but alterations were needed. The seamstress who was called into the dressing room moved quickly and quietly as she approached her work. She promptly knelt on the floor to check the hem. When she murmured "hello" I immediately caught an accent. Obviously she was from somewhere in the Middle East.

During my travels to Eastern Europe I had several distressing, even dangerous experiences; and through them I learned how much it meant to have someone smile and offer assistance. Thinking of that, I remembered that I had committed to extending kindness to any foreigners who might cross my path in America. This decision was the beginning of a particular partnership with God. Out of this partnership has come many memorable, wonderful experiences, and now I was about to enter into a wonderful dialogue with one whom God loved, Roxana.

As she began to pin my slacks I asked her where she was from. "You will *never* guess where I'm from," she replied in a cynical tone. I started naming countries. She was surprised that I was persisting. On the third attempt I guessed Afghanistan. She glanced up, and with the beginning of a smile and a whole lot more interest, she said, "Yes!"

I told her that I had long been interested in her country (these events were prior to September 11, 2001) and was especially concerned about the plight of women there. Then I began to ask her questions. That day in the dressing room Roxana and I had a dynamic conversation about some of her experiences.

God had been speaking to me about her country for years, and I had been listening. I have often prayed for the people, especially the women, who live there. I knew that Afghanistan was a poor, war-ravaged Muslim country where it was religiously, politically and socially correct to keep women "in their place." Sadly, for many Afghani women that assigned place was at the bottom of a weary, dispirited heap.

I left that day thanking God that finally I had met someone from that country. Yet I also felt sad about one comment Roxana made concerning how women are treated there. After telling me about the cultural and religious double standard that created a rift between her and her brother, she then clearly proclaimed her dislike of religion—any religion. In her mind all religions oppress women. My immediate impression was that it would take time for Roxana to soften enough to respond to Christian friendship, let alone the gospel message.

When I went to the store to pick up my clothes, I asked a sales representative to please call Roxana for me. When she answered the phone, I said "hello" and went on to reintroduce myself, not assuming that she would have remembered our encounter in the dressing room. To my surprise she assured me of her recollection with the pointed exclamation, "I'll *never* forget you as long as I live." Humbled, I said I just wanted to thank her for altering my clothes and ask about how things were going with her brother.

We talked for a few minutes, but on the drive back home I couldn't stop thinking about Roxana. I knew God was inviting me to pay attention. It suddenly clicked that I'd been praying for her country and now I had met a woman from there who had just said she would never forget me. As I was experiencing the pleasure of receiving such an unexpected compliment, God gently reminded me that he'd designed this encounter and had opened the door for a relationship to begin.

I was reminded of God's prompting the next time I arrived at the store and she again came into my dressing room for alterations. I told her that I had been thinking about her a great deal and would like to talk with her more about her experiences, if and when she was willing. She quickly agreed.

I accepted with delight Roxana's invitation to come to her house for our conversation. Her home was lovely, spacious, sparsely furnished and carefully kept. She extended herself to me in every conceivable way. As we sipped tea and settled around the kitchen table, she admitted that she'd never told her story to anyone—not even her own children.

There simply are not pages enough to tell Roxana's story. Here, remarriage is common after divorce. In Roxana's country, divorce is not easy for women, though under Islamic law a man can have up to four wives at one time. Roxana's mother was the second wife of her father who was a widower with seven sons, one of the wealthiest men in that country. Roxana never knew a home without tension; her stepbrothers were jealous of their father's new wife and his children by her and concerned about their inheritance. For Roxana, the tension was heightened by the fact that her parents told her that she was an unwanted child. (Birth control is not generally practiced.)

Roxana's mother treated her and her many siblings with studied neglect. The children sought but never received love or acceptance from their parents or each other. In her family, Roxana was used by siblings to bear the brunt of their frustrations. Because culturally it was shameful to express negative emotions, she had no outlet for the pain she bore.

She lived with her mother in a big, beautiful house surrounded by a common courtyard serving other homes for the families of her stepbrothers, for her father and for his next wife. Although he had sometimes expressed affection to Roxana and often invited her to join him for breakfast, his newest wife hated her, making the visits so painful that Roxana stayed away.

She was five years old when her father died and life became even more difficult. Her stepbrothers saw to it that there was less food and fewer privileges for her side of the family. Her mother was saddled with the powerlessness of being only a woman and now one of two wives. When she was nine, Roxana's mother died and things deteriorated further. Every day she worried about what would become of her. She was left in the hands of her hateful eldest stepbrother, an unenviable position for the youngest girl in a Muslim family consumed by the scramble for inheritance.

When she was fourteen, Roxana's sister arranged for her to be married to one of her husband's cousins, a man sixteen years her senior. Girls are often placed in arranged marriages, sometimes even before puberty. Her brother-in-law was increasing his power and authority in the family by bringing in another of his male relatives. This is a common practice. Roxana's prospective groom was an alcoholic, but her brother-in-law ignored the possible consequences of this, being concerned only for the ways he would benefit from this union. Her marriage was disastrous from the beginning. Her husband was often drunk, frequently unfaithful and always indifferent to her needs. Her duty was to submit to his every sexual demand, and very soon she was pregnant.

She lived in the home of her husband's family and was ruled over by a vicious mother-in-law. For the first time in her life she was required to cook and do household chores. Soon after the birth of her first daughter, she became pregnant again. Fourteen years and four daughters later, under intense political unrest, Roxana's husband fled with his family to America. They were politically safe but culturally and financially undone. Roxana found work as a seamstress and, thanks to her competence and intelligence, quickly advanced in her career.

Eventually her husband's drunkenness and mean-spirited indifference led her to divorce him. Those of her brothers who had also emigrated were infuriated by her boldness and punished her by withdrawing any semblance of family support. It took amazing fortitude, but she relocated herself and her children to Southern California. On her own, Roxana moved, secured work and supported and raised her children. When I met her, two of her daughters were in college, enjoying opportunities denied to their mother.

For over two hours Roxana talked intensely about important memories from her past. I paid attention with all the energy I had. She spoke slowly and with great feeling. I asked probing questions and suggested connections between things that she had not yet made, which she gladly welcomed. There were times in our conversation when my heart was so heavy with sadness that I cried and asked for a bit of time to process what she was sharing. That someone was finally listening to her story and giving her the attention she needed and deserved was very meaningful to her. It was meaningful to me to be invited into her confidence. I felt as though I was standing on holy ground, watching a woman uncover her soul.

William James said that the deepest principle in human nature is the craving to be appreciated,[4] and this proved true for Roxana. To listen with empathy is to demonstrate appreciation. After two hours of paying close attention, my neck ached, my back was as stiff as it has ever been, and my heart felt as though it had been hit by a freight train. I was exhausted.

We both needed a break, so I invited Roxana to lunch. As we were eating, she shared some details about her present life, and at this point our cultural differences evaporated. A male friend had come to her earlier that day, asking for a $2,000 loan. She was apprehensive. His track record of financial responsibility was shaky. As we talked about this, I helped her see that this was an *American* situation. Here, women do not necessarily heed the demands of men. I was able to help her see that she could tell her friend no. We role-played how to do it. Now we were simply two women sharing a culture and exercising options.

By the time lunch was finished, Roxana confided in me about something that she had done twenty-two years earlier, something for which she declared she "could never forgive herself," something she had never shared. In no way did her behavior approach the evil label she attached to it, but it was trapped in her mind and heart as such.

I was disturbed about this unnecessary burden she carried. With compassion I said, "Roxana, someday you are going to have to forgive yourself. I want to see you forgive yourself for this blunder. How about today?" As I reviewed her story and peeled away the label of evil, I watched the power of the past dissipate. Finally she was free, simply because she dared to share her life's worst moment with someone who listened with compassion and mercy.

Up to this point in our dialogue, I had not mentioned God. I had maintained my focus of listening to Roxana's story. Now *she* brought up the topic. She asked me about my feelings on religion. When I told her that I was a Christian, she pointed immediately to her goose-bumped-arms response. She somehow thought that I might be a Christian. She went on to tell me that at important junctures, after coming to America, God placed Christian women in her life who loved and supported her. She was touched by their acceptance and support; she had heard the claims of Christ and even read the Bible with them. Emotionally Roxana's resistance was melting.

Although I know that Muslims are firmly entrenched in their religion by tradition, culture and politics, now I was in the presence of a woman wearied by the weaknesses of that very system. I sensed from watching the expression on her face and listening to her appreciation of the Christian women she'd met that she was aware that genuine Christianity was good. I was concerned, though, about her experience with these Christians. They advised her and supported her through difficult circumstances, but they did not seem to truly know her. I was the first person to ever ask her to tell her story.

As she continued her story, I saw that not all of Roxana's experiences with Christianity had been positive. She had attended a Bible study where coercion was used. Someone demanded that she attend church regularly and donate money, and they required her children to accompany her. That's a lot of pressure on a single parent from a Muslim background. I tried to put myself in Roxana's place, and I felt her anger toward that kind of pressure.

I wasn't surprised to learn that Roxana left the Bible study, scared and scarred. Over the years she's developed sonar that detects hidden agendas. But there was hope. When she said something was missing in her life, I knew that God had been speaking to Roxana and that she had been listening. She understands that she has a spiritual vacancy in her heart, and compassionate Christians have helped her pay attention to her emptiness.

Evangelism happens when we partner with God by willingly placing our priorities within his and by participating with him in bringing his kingdom to this earth. When I thought about talking with Roxana about her life, I knew it was going to take considerable time and would involve a great deal of spiritual, emotional and intellectual energy. God does not force us to assume his priorities. I had to fight the temptation to do other important, or at least pressing, work. It was an immense struggle for me to move this direction. It was also an exhilarating experience to partner with God that day.

The last thing we did was pray together. We were sitting in my car in front of her house when I suggested it. I doubt she has ever done this before. It was a moving moment for both of us. God's presence was evident. My prayer is that it brought her one step closer to the time and place when she will meet Jesus. Despite the challenge of distance and time, our friendship continues. On one birthday I took her a gift. I talk with her occasionally and my approach is always the same: listen attentively, encourage her whenever I can and share those parts of my story with God that relate to her experience.

After the bombing in Afghanistan, I called her, knowing that if I were in her place, I would need someone to listen to my sadness and fear. As I write this, Roxana is trying to get a regular day off so that we can study the Bible together, and I am praying for other Christians in her area to come alongside us. I'm watching for God to call together a team of people who will love her into the kingdom of God.

## ENGAGE IN BEING EMPATHETIC

1. What insights in this chapter were useful to you?

2. How do you respond to the concept of being a partner with God in evangelism?

3. Read Acts 17:16-32. Luke wrote this account after watching it and also listening to Paul talk about it. Reread it aloud, using the emphasis Luke might have intended.

   a. If you had been Paul, what would have worked against your being empathetic in this situation?

   b. Explain what methods Paul used to listen to the Athenians before his formal address to the Areopagus.

   c. Using the definition of empathy given at the beginning of this chapter, how does Paul demonstrate empathy here?

d.  What other characteristics of Paul are in his presentation, and what can you learn from this?

4.  As you walk through this day, you will certainly encounter people with a story to tell. They might be sitting next to you in church next Sunday. How can you begin now to practice empathy with the unbelievers in your life?

Your answer may make an eternal difference to someone. Other things, important and good things, discouraged my developing a friendship with Roxana. Yet, there she was, in the middle of it all, willing to tell me her story. Is there a more effective tool of evangelism? Surely not.

# 9

# REFLECTIVE

## YOUR HISTORY IS ON YOUR SIDE

*There is one art of which every man should be a master—*
*the art of reflection.*

SAMUEL COLERIDGE

*Taking the five loaves and the two fish and looking up to heaven,*
*he gave thanks and broke the loaves.*
*Then he gave them to his disciples to set before the people.*
*He also divided the two fish among them all.*
*The number of the men*
*who had eaten was five thousand.*

MARK 6:41, 44

CHRISTIANS become reflective as they pause and look back on their life experiences to see how God's redemptive presence has shaped their lives. It's especially helpful in evangelism to reflect on how God brought us to salvation, what we were comfortable with in that process and what we were not. When we have identified what worked for us, then we can confidently use what we've learned to evangelize our non-Christian friends.

Picture two sardines on a tray. Now add brown, coarse bread to the tray. Jesus broke two such fish and five loaves of peasant barley bread and then miraculously multiplied it to feed five thousand people. It's noteworthy that this is the only miracle other than the resurrection included in all four Gospels.

Now place yourself in that scene as the boy who, according to John, had the food. Put the story into your context. Your heavenly Father has sent you off for the day. He has packed your bag. Your life story is your sustenance, the food you have to offer to Jesus to feed others. You may feel as Andrew did about the little boy's lunch: "But how far will [it] go among so many?" (Jn 6:9). As the miracle reveals, this really isn't your problem. It's up to God to multiply it. Your job is to offer it to Jesus to break open and feed others. In his hands your history becomes a feast for those who are spiritually hungry!

## WHEN LITTLE BECOMES AMPLE

The Gospel accounts reveal that the feeding of the five thousand occurred in an isolated place. This crowd had been listening to Jesus, who had been speaking to them out of compassion because they were "like sheep without a shepherd" (Mk 6:34). The hour was late.

Have you ever been tired and hungry in a deserted place with no restaurant in sight? I remember one such spot. I was on a train, crossing over the Hungarian border from Romania. This was when there was a Berlin Wall and we had to endure tedious border checks throughout Eastern Europe.

We had forgotten to get Hungarian visas (a sign of freedom taken for granted), so my traveling companion and I got bumped off our train in the middle of the night. We had to go to the border stop where they issued visas. At dawn we rode on a milk train filled with rural peasants (I remember wiping vomit off my seat before sitting down), followed by a long walk to the border. We were carrying our luggage along a deserted road. It was hot and it was about three o'clock in the afternoon. We hadn't eaten since our meager breakfast. Fatigue was pressing in, as was trepidation about uncertainties we would surely find at the border.

Then, out of nowhere, a friendly, curious Romanian peasant woman appeared and stopped us. She offered water from a tin cup sunk into a community bowl, not clean by American standards. We were desperate enough to gratefully drink it without question and eat the wormy, unwashed apples offered to us.

From this experience I can better imagine Mark's crowd. I think the crowd resembles the people without Jesus in our world today. If we could look into the hearts and minds of the people whizzing by us on the freeway, standing in line at the post office, sitting beside us in the movies or at the baseball field, we would likely see people desperate for a slice of good news. They want good news that's reliable—indispensable truth that remains with them when the world turns upside down.

The story of Jesus' feeding the five thousand captures what I have come to understand about how God wants to use our stories. We may think they are meager fare. But God satisfied the hunger of five thousand people with five loaves of bread and two sardines. In Western culture today a whopping majority of the population does not accept the Bible as true or the gospel as necessary. This same population, however, does accept our experiences as valid. Evangelism involves knowing our own stories well enough that we can relate them to the experiences of our unbelieving audience. I have yet to hear two people give the same testimony of how God is working in their lives, and I have never heard a boring one.

## OUR HISTORY WITH EVANGELISM

Reflecting on how we were evangelized strengthens our confidence in how we can, in turn, evangelize others. When I hear stories of how friends came to Christ and how they evangelize, I notice that invariably we tend to evangelize others in ways similar to the way we ourselves were evangelized. We learn from mistakes done to us, and we tend to copy what worked in bringing us to Jesus. The important thing at this point is to sort all of this out; decide how to keep and effectively use what we already know but may have temporarily forgotten.

Begin with the permanent, invincible fact that God has given each of us a distinctive personality and different talents, spiritual gifts, experiences and preferences. Go back to the lists you made in chapter three, "Focused." Stay with your discoveries. You have thoughts and feelings nobody else processes in quite the same way. Others, especially non-Christians, need to hear what you have to say. You have a point of view that's irreplaceable—a way of experiencing and expressing things that God wants to use.

When I started reflecting, I remembered an experience from when I was seven years old. We lived in Illinois and Grandma's home had a breezeway, a room connecting the garage with the house. It was a sunny, narrow room we used to sit in during the summer. In the winter it would serve as a buffer between the cold outside and the warmth inside.

On this particular afternoon I was sitting in the breezeway reading, and Grandma came in from the garage with a vine that had crept in through a crack. It was about a foot long but it was spindly and almost white. I found it scary to look at. Grandma recognized this and sat down beside me. She gently explained that the vine looked unnatural because it wasn't getting sunlight, the very thing that would provide the chlorophyll needed to turn it green. It was just a shadow of the vine it could have been if it had been exposed to the sun. She then went on to liken the vine to our lives and what they're like without Christ.

Her words stayed tucked in my soul for the next sixteen years. When I came to know Christ, they became gloriously accurate. From this I learned to take whatever visual aid was at hand and use it to share Jesus. One day I even used a simple napkin and drew a sketch of what the gospel accomplishes for us and persuaded a woman to receive Christ.

Another milestone in my understanding of evangelism occurred a year later, when I was eight. On a warm, summer night, my sister and I had gone to church, and we were playing outside with our friends after the service was over. The next morning we were leaving with Mother and our two brothers to go to Virginia to be reunited with our father. He and mother were turning over a new leaf. I was looking forward to this new experience. Conversely, Aunt Ellen was deeply concerned. Add to that, she tended to approach everything on a strictly cognitive level. She thought she had figured out what she could do to help my sister, Ellen, and me.

Right then and there, she brought us over to the pastor and explained that we were leaving for Virginia in the morning and that she would like for us to receive Christ before our departure. Pastor George began asking us whether we knew Jesus was the Son of God and that he died for our sins. I remember feeling ashamed and embarrassed. At that time and in that area of the country, all were supposed to be Christians. Add to that backdrop the reality that I was at a stage where peer acceptance was crucial. All I could think about was that my friends would judge me. (My sister, incidentally, did not find this uncomfortable at all.) When our pastor led us in a prayer, I simply mouthed the words. I was caught between pleasing my pastor and being embarrassed in front of my friends.

Having had such an awkward experience of evangelism, I try to be aware of what would embarrass an unbeliever, and I intentionally try not to do anything that would make an unbeliever feel unnecessarily uncomfortable. Today I see that balmy summer's evening as one of my most valuable learning experiences. I don't want to be the cause of anyone feeling the way I did that night.

Yet another event happened in Greenup, Illinois, when I was barely a teenager. I was sitting at a café and saw three young women get up from their table to leave. I noticed that instead of leaving a tip, they left an evangelistic pamphlet. I was embarrassed by this and wondered whether this act was actually fair. Again I felt uncomfortable. Evangelism should be done in a spirit of generosity. If the young women had left a generous tip along with the pamphlet, my reaction would have been different. Today I hold this firm conviction: if we make mistakes in evangelism, let them be on the side of generosity.

About ten years later I was having coffee in the restaurant of our local department store. I was twenty-two then, a bride working at the store for Christmas money. By now I had shed all vestiges of Christianity, and I was talking about it with a pastor's wife I had just met in the restaurant. Finally she graciously intervened and questioned why, if I had actually shed Christianity, I was still talking about it. I don't remember my response. It probably involved an excuse coupled with a quick exit. I was terribly unsettled by her observation because I knew it was true. I was not unsettled by her; she was far too courteous for me to find fault with her. From this startling event, I learned that it's possible and necessary to state the truth in ways that don't detract from its message.

Two years later I was sitting in an English composition class in which the professor was using existentialism as a basis for all our writing. Our class was deeply involved in a discussion about the nature of existentialism, tossing our opinions around to each other as though they were facts. From the back of the room a woman offered an intelligent, reasonable and logical comment. She spoke with calmness and objectivity. In my mind, completely unbidden, came the thought, *This woman is a Christian.* It turned out that her name was Lois and, well, you know the rest of the story.

I learned two things from that class discussion. First, God prepares our minds and hearts for truth. He had prepared me to meet Lois and recognize the quality of her character. Second, evangelism is more than words about Jesus. One of our most effective witnessing tools in a completely secular environment is how we present ourselves. Lois offered what to me were clearly the most intelligent comments, and she did this with a winsome attitude. I wanted to hear more. I wanted to get to know her. Today I consider my attitudes are as important as what I say. I aim for congruency. I also interact with people on the assumption that God has prepared them even when the evidence may not support that assumption.

The next important experience in my life came a few years later at a restaurant. By now our second son, Nathan, had been born. He was only a week old when his doctors began to suspect he was highly allergic. He cried most of the time, and we often couldn't make him comfortable. He felt miserable, and we were exhausted from taking care of him. On this evening we had decided to go out for dinner. We reasoned that we could make Nathan happy for at least forty-five minutes. No sooner had we ordered the food than Nathan began to fuss. We tried holding him, walking him, rocking him, giving him a bottle, giving him a pacifier, ignoring him—nothing worked! The food came and we were trying to gobble it down quickly so we could escape and spare the other poor diners who were subjected to the noise they neither expected nor enjoyed.

Yet one of these people kept smiling at us with understanding— an older woman who probably saw our predicament through the eyes of her own experience. She got up from her booth, came and put her arm around me and asked if she could hold our baby while we ate. I gave all the expected responses, mostly centered on the insistence that we didn't want to impose. She quietly and kindly persisted. We finally gave in, with the thought that it probably wouldn't work. This woman had a deep reservoir of peace and love that settled in on Nathan. She used no words about Jesus, but I was certain then that she was a Christian. This remains for me one of the kindest acts I've ever experienced, and I'm now convinced that human kindness is one of our most effective tools in evangelism.

These situations and the events with Lois I've written about earlier are the experiences that God used to shape the way I evangelize. I don't think I took time to consciously reflect on them in the early years when I was sharing Christ, but they clearly marked my approach. Later I looked back over my history and saw these experiences with new eyes. Reflecting back, I see how God perfectly designed them for me. In my pre-Christian days I was too self-absorbed to be kind, too isolated to be sensitive, too brash to be understanding.

Your evangelism experiences are perfect for you, but you need to collect them, polish them with thought and prayer and learn the scope of what God has done in saving you just the way he did.

## RECLAIMING METHODS

You may have rejected some methods you now need to use. Perhaps some of your assumptions can be turned around. Something like this happened to me in an unlikely place and in an unusual way.

I had pretty much decided in Greenup, Illinois, that I wasn't comfortable handing out pamphlets to strangers, and I have seldom done it. I had just finished a speaking engagement. I parked near the store and was about to enter the shopping mall through one of its doors when I stepped into the restroom at Saks Fifth Avenue. To leave the restroom I had to go through a spacious outer room, where I stopped to reapply lipstick. An elegant older woman was seated near the mirror and talking to her daughter-in-law about how meaningless her life had become. She went into lots of detail, including how concerned her husband was about her. Her frail voice cut right into my heart. When I left the restroom, she was still talking.

As I moved through the store, God began to deal with me. I had a tract titled "How to Have a Meaningful Life" in my purse. It had been there for a while, and it was well worn, but now I felt God wanted me to give the pamphlet to this woman. At first I balked. After all, she was a complete stranger and I didn't pass out pamphlets to strangers. This was Saks Fifth Avenue, for heaven's sake. *People don't behave that way in this store,* I groaned inwardly. But I was literally stricken with her despairing conversation, so I forced myself back to the restroom, partly hoping she had left. She hadn't. I knew what I had to do. I simply explained that this is not my usual manner with strangers, but that I had a pamphlet that I believed could bring her a different understanding of her life. I apologized for its worn exterior in response to the daughter-in-law's noted alarm. I managed a weak smile as I bolted for the door.

I held this woman and her daughter-in-law before God in prayer not just that day, but in the days that followed and even today as I retrieve this memory. At first I just prayed for her to read the pamphlet with an open mind and heart. Then my prayer focused on God bringing other believers into her life to minister to her and help her on her way to meaningful faith.

Eternity will show me the end of this story.

## COMPASSIONATE REFLECTION

As we reflect on our lives, as we see ourselves with adult fairness, we learn to be kind to ourselves. When I was three years old, my mother said something so horrible to me that I repressed it for thirty-five years. In all fairness, my mother was drunk. Desperation pulled her there. I told my counselor that my mother had said something awful to me, though I could not recall what. This was my oft-repeated mantra, to which my counselor calmly assured me that when it was time, I would. When I finally did recall it, I realized two things. First, in response to that painful phrase I had been driven all my life to prove her wrong and I was tired of the fight. Second, if I was going to get past this, I was going to have to be kind to myself. I didn't know how to do this. I had to ask God to teach me.

I went to my husband and a few Christian friends sympathetic to my growth and told them what I was going through. They prayed for me. They brought flowers and dinners. They sent cards. God helped me then. He's still helping me today. And he's helping other people through my experience. I don't have a number for how many people have shared their version of a similar story with me. I encountered a statement by John Watson during this season that's stuck: "Be kind; everyone you meet is fighting a hard battle."[1] I believe it. Life is difficult, and to think otherwise is to try to fool ourselves.

Life experience has shown me this truth, which is verified by social scientists: our childhood sets the stage for how we act out the rest of our lives. What we experienced as children determines the props on the stage of our lives. In different acts of our play we can change the props. We can paint them, reupholster them or change their position in the room—but they remain onstage with us. Throughout our lives we will face problems, the roots of which go back to our childhood. My fear of failure looks different now than it did when I was twenty. When I pause to reflect on what I'm feeling, I can trace the origin of my response. I can then remember God's faithfulness to me in previous times of fear; I can deal with it and be released. We can learn to consider these hard times of reflection as friends that lead us to a more significant life and ministry with others.

Each experience we have had—regardless of how embarrassing, sad, shameful or even seemingly insignificant—has the potential to be used redemptively by God in the people whose paths cross ours. If the people who came to that Galilean hillside with their meager and simple food had refused to relinquish it to the disciples, we wouldn't have the marvelous miracle of Jesus feeding a multitude. Sometimes I imagine the people on that hillside coming to us and encouraging us by saying, "Give your stories away and get ready for God to use them beyond your wildest hopes and dreams!"

## JAMES'S STORY

I met James because he worked in my favorite art gallery. We had only one surface-level chat the first time I was in his gallery. At that time I commented on how much I appreciated dealing with him. Mutual understanding mushroomed from that first meeting. Later he became the manager of the gallery and did an outstanding job. It was so much fun to have him walk me around the gallery—such a joy to congratulate him on a job well done. I asked him about his twelve-year-old son, Tony. At that time I was writing a study on the Ten Commandments, and James was sharing something he had done for Tony that was so appropriate that I found myself talking about the commandment "Honor your father and your mother" (Ex 20:12). James turned to me and confessed that he had a spiritual problem and that he thought I was the one who could help him.

Seldom have I experienced this kind of openness. I was so surprised that I thought I hadn't heard him correctly. I asked him to repeat what he had just said. Yes, I had heard him correctly. He then went on to tell me his sincere struggle with the notion that surely there had to be more than just one way to God. I could see this was a painful issue for James. I also sensed that it was only one of many issues he was struggling with. I asked if he'd be willing to enter into a long dialogue about spiritual issues. James eagerly accepted. He knew the complexities of his situation. My willingness to take the time to talk about it seemed to relieve him.

Our first meeting took place soon after that over dinner. For this dialogue I wanted us to be on equal footing. I wanted to understand his perspective and, equally important, I wanted him to understand mine. So I suggested that we describe for each other where we were on our spiritual journey. I volunteered to go first to give him an example of what I meant.

I had a reason to share first. I thought perhaps James was a homosexual, and I wanted to share some things about my childhood that would be difficult to share—honest, but costly. I was hoping to set an example for him, so I was completely transparent, weaving throughout my story how God had met me in distressing and intense places. Since I thought James might be dealing with sexual issues, I talked about my experiences of being sexually abused as a child, the issues I had to work through and how God's comforting presence provided me with the strength I needed to climb out of that dark hole.

In turn, James shared the physical and emotional abuse he endured at the hand of his father. He talked of his religious background and of his marriage that ended in divorce after twenty-one years. He spoke of the many ways he tried to save that marriage, including joining the Jehovah's Witnesses with his wife. He was a faithful Witness most of his married life. He enjoyed telling me about his son, Tony, obviously the most important person in his life. He described his mother, a close second to Tony in his affections. He talked about his sexual conflict, being torn between heterosexual and homosexual identities. Contrary to the stereotype many hold, he has only had one partner, has never been to a gay bar and recognizes many weaknesses in the gay community. James's pull toward homosexuality began in his childhood.

Now we both had a context for our dialogue, which, to date, remains unfinished. The lines of communication are still open even though he has reunited with his partner. He has told Tony, now fourteen, that he is gay. He has told his father, and that relationship appears severed.

Is God finished with James? Not at all. He still clings to our friendship. I've been honest with him and have simply stated (I hope without a hint of judgment) that I think he has made an unwise choice and I am his friend for life. If I understand the Bible correctly, what James has chosen will not work. I pray faithfully for James. I share how God is working in my life. We see each other as often as we can. He's an only child and I know that our friendship means a great deal to him. It also means a lot to me. I don't know how or when God will become real to James. All I know for certain is that God has not removed my desire for that to happen.

## OUR HISTORY WITH GOD

The world doesn't need one more superficial evangelist, another Christian who speaks without reflection. We don't live in a one-dimensional world; we don't interact with one-dimensional people. Reflecting on how we were evangelized provides an essential move away from surface evangelism.

Let's be honest—it's difficult in our world, where tolerance ranks as a top virtue, to declare the gospel of Jesus. Because of this, it's vital that we Christians become comfortable with the way we will be able to evangelize. When people take the time to reflect on their evangelism experiences, their common reaction is, "I can do *this*!"

Our experiences with evangelism aren't the only things we learn to reflect on. Scripture is filled with references to believers reflecting on God's ongoing work on their behalf. We'll be looking at this ongoing reflection, and the insight it brings, in the next chapter. These truths of our spiritual life are what unbelievers need to hear. Such realities are much more palatable than some sort of fake or prepackaged façade that doesn't include our sweat and pain.

---

## ENGAGE IN BECOMING REFLECTIVE

---

1. What was useful to you in this chapter?

2. What opportunities for growth might you find as you look at your life through the selective lens of God's redemptive work?

3. Read the account of Paul's conversion given to King Agrippa in Acts 25:23—26:18 with the understanding that Paul had many years to formulate his testimony. Notice the way he is evangelizing Agrippa. This testimony is considered a model defense of Christianity.

   Here's the context: Paul is a Roman citizen and wants to appeal to the Roman emperor to receive his freedom to continue his missionary work. Up to this point he has been ferociously opposed by the Jews, but as a Roman citizen he has certain rights, one of which is being protected. Agrippa ruled parts of Palestine, was familiar with the Hebrew religion and was Paul's last interview and last hope for actually getting to Rome. For now we will look at only the first part of Paul's testimony and will complete it in chapter ten.

   a. Agrippa was acutely aware of the Jewish religion. What points about Judaism did Paul include in his testimony, and why do you suppose he chose these?

   b. On a scale of one to ten, with ten being highest, what level of intensity does Paul's presentation to Agrippa have?

   c. How does that level of intensity square with Paul's own conversion experience?

    d. Explain from Paul's example why it's important in evangelism for Christians—especially those who became Christians as children and those who have known Jesus for many years—to reflect on how we came to Christ and how he is an ongoing source of strength.

4. Identify which of the categories below best fits your background, and answer the questions that apply.

    a. It could be that you were brought up in a Christian home and you became a Christian as a child. You will need to ask yourself questions like these: What characteristics of Christianity modeled by your family led you to your adult commitment? What were the benefits of being raised in that home? What were the benefits of being raised in a church? How did Jesus become real to you as an adult? How can you avoid the "perfect Christian family" stereotype when you have an opportunity to share your story with an unbeliever? (You may feel that you need to avoid talking about your Christian background with seekers. I don't think this is the case. We hear a great deal about the brokenness in the world, and we need to hear far more from the people who were reared in a healthy Christian home.)

    b. Suppose yours was an unhappy Christian home. What were the memorable experiences that God used to bring you to Jesus? What struggles did you face? What were the in-spite-of issues that you had to work through? What were the distorted pictures of God that you had to set right? How did you do it? Countless people are waiting for your slice of the good news.

    c. Some of us will have been raised in a different religion entirely. What was it about that religion that bothered you enough for you to change your belief system? What was lacking? What attracted you to Jesus? How did you go about making the transition to Christianity? What were your biggest challenges and your greatest surprises?

d. Perhaps, like many of us today, you were raised in a nonreligious home. What were your parents like? How were they effective parents? How were they ineffective? How did they shape your understanding of God? What holes were created in you as you grew up in an unspiritual environment? What did you go through to become a person of faith?

e. If none of the above categories fit, establish one that's right for you. For example, two of them loosely apply to me. My religious background was confusing. My parents weren't religious. The only time I saw my mother pray was when she was in an alcoholic stupor. But my grandparents and my aunt were Christians. Here are some questions you might consider if your background is like mine: What word would you use to describe your religious experience in your family? What created your openness to Jesus? What challenges did you have to overcome in giving him your life? What were your experiences in being evangelized?

5. Retrieve your memories of being evangelized. Try to remember what you thought and how you felt in each situation. Figure out how your experiences affect your own practice of witnessing and evangelism. Articulate your own evangelism style. Then go out into the world, determined to share Jesus in a way that has proved effective for you. See yourself as a little boy or girl with two sardines and five little loaves of bread. Jesus is going to feed hungry people with what you have to offer. Let your imagination soar.

# 10
# INSIGHTFUL

## UNCOVERING THE INSIDE STORY

*The situation today is:*
*Lots of knowledge, but little understanding.*
*Lots of means, but little meaning.*
*Lots of know-how, but little know-why.*
*Lots of sight, but little insight.*

ROBERT SHORT

*Everyone who heard him was amazed at his understanding*
*and his answers. . . . And Jesus grew in wisdom*
*and stature, and in favor with God and men.*

LUKE 2:47, 52

**INSIGHT** is the power of seeing into a situation or into someone's life. Insight follows reflection. It's a necessary quality in evangelism because the gospel of Jesus ultimately deals with issues of the heart and the true nature of what every human being experiences.

More than anything else, Bill wanted his non-Christian family members and friends to come into a personal relationship with Jesus. His attempts to communicate this to them were ineffective. Bill simply didn't know how to have a significant spiritual dialogue with the people most important to him. Yes, they knew he was a Christian, but they didn't know why that was so important to him. Bill had trouble articulating this, even to himself.

When Bill and I talked about this, I began to ask him questions about his background. I discovered that Bill hadn't reflected on some of the important events of his childhood even though they played a significant role in forming his personality. For example, both of his parents had a deep faith that helped them face difficulties and that provided a moral framework for how to rear their children. Every week Bill's parents took him to church, and for the most part his Sunday school teachers were excellent role models. During his high school years a couple of adults in the youth group really helped him through some rough times. As it turned out, Bill's only sister was sick with a debilitating and terminal illness. This affected the whole family system. Sometimes Bill was afraid, sometimes he was angry, and at other times he thought, *Why, God?*

If we want to tell the people we love about Jesus, then we have to be able to see inside our stories and discover what they mean spiritually. If Bill wants to evangelize his family and friends, he will need to comb through the important events in his life and pray for God to give him insight about what they mean and how they have shaped his life. Bill was in his mid-thirties when he took up this challenge. You may be older or younger, but I'm sure of this: you have many dynamic stories to tell of how God has worked in your life. It's never too late to uncover these stories. Today is a good day to begin.

## INSIGHT AND GOSPEL STORIES

We can learn a lot about successful evangelism by watching the way my young friends Cari and Phil approached their relationship. They became acquainted while working on a dude ranch in Colorado. Although they were quite attracted to each other, they approached their relationship with caution. Both were raised in broken homes, leaving them sensitive to the need to take time developing a true picture of each other and their relationship prior to committing to marriage. This process demanded prayerful consideration, vulnerability, transparency and, ultimately, trust.

Herein lie the parallels for modern-day evangelists: We are seeking to bring people to Jesus and lead them toward a life of serving him as King forever. Such an approach only happens over time. It requires both the Christian and his non-Christian friend to look inside each other. Only then can they develop an appreciation for one another that, in turn, moves them further along in their understanding of one another. The more the believer learns, the easier he finds it to love the one still searching. In essence, insight moves us toward love. It's equally important to be transparent with the nonbeliever, for then the believer proves his trustworthiness. Transparency from all parties involved plays a major role in persuading an unbeliever to give his or her life to Christ.

One mark of the spiritually mature is that they "by constant use have trained themselves to distinguish good from evil" (Heb 5:14). We grow in insight as we listen to and observe our unbelieving friends. We discover what they are inwardly grappling with, and we begin to draw the connection between how parts of our own story relate to them. Sooner or later a day will come when we will have an opportunity to tell our story. When that happens, we can use the insight we've gained to custom fit our story to the needs of our unbelieving friends.

It is encouraging to know that insight is a spiritual quality—one that Jesus possessed, one that he *increased* in.[1] And it is also important to know that his insights drew favor from his contemporaries (Lk

4:36-37). For purposes of evangelism, insight takes on the additional meaning of *understanding in the spiritual realm.* Since salvation is an inside job, it makes sense to cultivate an inside understanding of ourselves and of our unbelieving friends.

As you have reflected on your own story, you've begun collecting insights. Now apply your insight to the stories of your unbelieving friends. Listen to them with empathy. See how your story fits with theirs. Begin telling your story as opportunities arise. All the while keep in mind that you're moving toward the appropriate time to be more intentional, to actually share the gospel. Your gospel story is simply your story plus the gospel. It isn't appropriate to give your gospel story before your friends are ready to receive it. I've found it best to wait until my non-Christian friends express an interest in hearing it. An example of this is the story that concludes this chapter.

## SAFETY AND SEQUENCE

In evangelism the principles of "safety and sequence" open doors that can be opened in no other way. We must strive to make our relationship a safe place for unbelievers to disclose their hearts. This means we sequence what we say. For example, imagine that you are giving a dinner party for a special friend. You would probably begin with appetizers, then move to salad, then bring out the main course and finally serve dessert. In evangelism we begin with casual friendship, then witness on a level that's safe for our friend. As the relationship develops in depth, our witnessing moves deeper with each level that's exposed.

Insight develops in the witnessing phase. Giving the gospel is serving the main course. Training a new convert to serve Jesus as Lord is the perfect finishing touch to the meal. If we share the gospel too quickly, it may leave people confused and possibly turn them away. Insight gained through practice and experience will show us when it's necessary and appropriate to share our gospel story.

The gospel is presented most powerfully in the context of an unbeliever's need and in light of your own experience of God's having

met a similar need in you. We can learn how to share our stories so
that they are completely different, depending on the need we are addressing. And even though the story varies with each telling, *each
story is still true!* There's enormous breadth in your human story—
God has seen to that. My testimony to someone dealing with an ad-
diction is completely different from my testimony to someone with a
terminal illness. Both stories are true, but they are quite different.

We can't go far in talking about experience without coming face to
face with need. Unbelievers have to recognize their need for salvation before they can receive it. As we develop a trusting friendship
with our unbelieving friends, it's possible that we will see their needs
even before they do. It's safe, for them and for you, to test your insights with them: "It sounds to me as though this is an area of need
for you. Do I understand you correctly?"

There comes a moment when our witnessing will lead to the point
at which giving the gospel (good news) is appropriate and necessary.
Paul explains the content of the good news we are to articulate to our
unbelieving friends like this in 1 Corinthians 15:1-8, below. (My commentary is given within the brackets.)

> Now, brothers, I want to remind you of the gospel I preached to you,
> which you received and on which you have taken your stand: . . . that
> Christ died for our sins according to the Scriptures [Jesus came, as a ful-
> fillment of biblical prophecy to die for our sins], that he was buried
> [Jesus did indeed die, signaling to us that his dealing with sin was com-
> plete], that he was raised on the third day according to the Scriptures
> [Jesus rose from the dead as a sign of his triumphant victory over sin],
> and that he appeared to Peter, and then to the Twelve. After that, he ap-
> peared to more than five hundred of the brothers at the same time. . . .
> Then he appeared to James, then to all the apostles, and last of all he ap-
> peared to me also [Jesus repeatedly showed himself to believers after
> the resurrection verifying that it was a true and historic event].

What we have to keep in mind here is that Paul was presenting the
gospel to Christians. His introduction to them reminded them of

their need to stand firm in the gospel. Such an introduction would not, of course, make sense to our unbelieving friends.

It's a challenge when people see themselves as not being sinners or as having missed out on God's plan. The gospel today is being offered to them in a society that has, on the whole, abandoned absolutes in favor of moral relativity. In addition to that bias, most nonbelievers are highly suspect of formal presentations and any approach that seems canned.

Given this, how are we supposed to move from witnessing to intentionally sharing the gospel? The apostle Paul offers us a highly relevant model.

## PAUL PRESENTS THE GOSPEL TO KING AGRIPPA

In Acts 26 we read of how Paul told his gospel story to King Agrippa. Here we discover that telling God's story has two essential elements: what God has done and how we have responded to it. I began giving my testimony before I knew most of my story because, due to the pain of remembering my childhood, I had blocked most of it out. Nevertheless, God used my testimony and people started giving their lives to Jesus because they saw a change in me. As God began to bring my memories to the surface, I was too ashamed of my background to use it in my testimony.

Sadly, I was also afraid church people would misjudge me or attach a label that would brand me for life. It was in the fleshing out of this story through Christian friends, counseling and intensive journal workshops that God's story finally emerged with power and dignity. I then had to dare to use it. Once I truly understood that it was really God's story I was telling, I became willing to share it because I yearned for others to know what God could do for them.

Given our twenty-first-century audience, how do we describe what God has done and how we have reacted to it? Using Paul as our model we'll look at the content of his speech and adjust it to today's audience without tampering with its integrity. Let's take a look at how Paul begins in Acts 26:2-3.

> King Agrippa, I consider myself fortunate to stand before you today
> as I make my defense against all the accusations of the Jews, and espe-
> cially so because you are well acquainted with all the Jewish customs
> and controversies. Therefore, I beg you to listen to me patiently.

In this introduction Paul demonstrates his mastery over social
skills. Agrippa assumed the position of king of Palestine when his father died. Palestine was occupied by the Romans during a decadent
period of their history, and Agrippa reflected that decadence by living in an incestuous relationship with his sister, Bernice. But, as we
say in today's vernacular, Paul didn't "go there." He refused to touch
that issue. Neither did he spurn Agrippa for his dubious past. He
simply began by pointing out Agrippa's credentials. He sculpts his
testimony to meet his audience, reflecting his understanding of
Agrippa's context and personal need.

> The Jews all know the way I have lived ever since I was a child, from the
> beginning of my life in my own country, and also in Jerusalem. They
> have known me for a long time and can testify, if they are willing, that
> according to the strictest sect of our religion, I lived as a Pharisee. And
> now it is because of my hope in what God has promised our fathers that
> I am on trial today. This is the promise our twelve tribes are hoping to
> see fulfilled as they earnestly serve God day and night. O king, it is be-
> cause of this hope that the Jews are accusing me. Why should any of you
> consider it incredible that God raises the dead? (Acts 26:4-8)

In the preceding generation of evangelists the emphasis was on
God's being personal. Paul demonstrates this with Agrippa, who was
familiar with the Jewish religion. Non-Christians today tenaciously
cling to their individuality, and they are enormously confused about
God. While we Christians know that God is personal, we face great
challenges in using this approach to reach people who readily assume
that their own personalized brand of God is acceptable. Knowing this,
it seems reasonable to approach them with the truth that God is the
Creator who made us and who has a claim on our lives.

You can see how Paul's testimony to Agrippa models this. He

shares his Jewish credentials and how he is on trial "because of my hope in what God has promised our fathers." He goes on to imply that he belongs to God and must live in light of that. The next part of Paul's story is intriguing from a contemporary vantage point because it uncovers the nature of sin.

> I too was convinced that I ought to do all that was possible to oppose the name of Jesus of Nazareth. And that is just what I did in Jerusalem. On the authority of the chief priests I put many of the saints in prison, and when they were put to death, I cast my vote against them. (Acts 26:9-10)

By saying, "I too was convinced," Paul establishes that he took ownership of his own life. The words that follow reveal that this decision led to more problems:

> Many a time I went from one synagogue to another to have them punished, and I tried to force them to blaspheme. In my obsession against them, I even went to foreign cities to persecute them. (Acts 26:11)

His words show us that when we push God out, we live in a constant struggle, which affects our relationships with others. We need not try to convince our contemporaries that we live in a world of broken relationships. In this simple verse Paul describes what happens when "I myself" dictates behavior. He was obsessed which led to further aggressive behavior. Paul is honest here without hyperbole, and he makes his point with minimal words.

Paul doesn't leave Agrippa with an unfinished story. He moves right on to talk about how Christ cleaned up the mess he had made with his life. The emphasis here is on Jesus: he is not dead; he is alive to help us with the problems we create.

> On one of these journeys I was going to Damascus with the authority and commission of the chief priests. About noon, O king, as I was on the road, I saw a light from heaven, brighter than the sun, blazing around me and my companions. We all fell to the ground, and I heard a voice saying to me in Aramaic, "Saul, Saul, why do you persecute me? It is hard for you to kick against the goads."

Then I asked, "Who are you, Lord?"

"I am Jesus, whom you are persecuting," the Lord replied. "Now get up and stand on your feet. I have appeared to appoint you as a servant and as a witness of what you have seen of me and what I will show you. I will rescue you from your own people and from the Gentiles. I am sending you to them to open their eyes and turn them from darkness to light, and from the power of Satan to God, so that they may receive forgiveness of sins and a place among those who are sanctified by faith in me." (Acts 26:12-18)

Now Paul goes on to illustrate that we need to respond to what Jesus offers. For starters, we need to place our faith in Christ, acknowledging this step as vital to being made right with God the Father, whom we have so deeply wronged. Second, we need to decide not to live for ourselves anymore and instead to commit to following God's leadership in submission, trust and obedience.

See how Paul gets this message across in Acts 26:19-23.

So then, King Agrippa, I was not disobedient to the vision from heaven. First to those in Damascus, then to those in Jerusalem and in all Judea, and to the Gentiles also, I preached that they should repent and turn to God and prove their repentance by their deeds. That is why the Jews seized me in the temple courts and tried to kill me. But I have had God's help to this very day, and so I stand here and testify to small and great alike. I am saying nothing beyond what the prophets and Moses said would happen—that the Christ would suffer and, as the first to rise from the dead, would proclaim light to his own people and to the Gentiles.

Paul points out that Jesus died, rose from the dead and lives now: "I have had God's help to this very day, and so I stand here and testify."

Our testimonies should model this concise proclamation. The result will be a compelling account that leaves listeners asking for more.

### SEVEN COMMON, CONTEMPORARY FELT NEEDS FOR THE GOSPEL

David Henderson has identified seven modern problems that create a need for salvation, I have adapted these and provided my own commentary.[2] Read them and then begin combing through your own history. You will probably find pieces of these felt needs tucked somewhere in your story. Contemplate how you might incorporate those fragments into your own gospel presentation.

*Alienation from others.* The breakdown of a family destroys the classroom that God designed for teaching us how to get along with others. As a result, many of us don't understand how to resolve conflict. From our families we go out in the world, to work, to school, to the gym and to other places where relationships form. Not the least of these relationships is marriage. We discover that these relationships often involve struggle. We feel frustrated and, too often, alone.

When have *you* felt alienated from others and how did God undertake to restore your relationship with them? How could you mold your testimony according to that need? How could you present the gospel in this story?

*Bad and unfair experiences.* You would be hard pressed to go far with people without running up against the problem of troublesome experiences. We have a keen sense of justice, especially when it comes to how we are treated. Bad and unfair experiences happen when we're sinned against. They also happen when we sin against others. Or when terrorists drop a bomb. Or when a tidal wave wipes out an island in the Pacific. Insurance companies label natural catastrophes "acts of God," though that may be mostly a misnomer given the fallen nature of the physical world (see Gen 3:14-19; Rom 8:21-22). Whatever you label them, these experiences hurt. Through them we lose innocence, trust, confidence and safety—things we hold most dear.

What bad or unfair experiences have you gone through that you can use in a testimony to someone who can't seem to get beyond this problem? Figure out how to fit the gospel into your story.

*Conflict of integrity.* I don't know anyone who hasn't experienced a gap between what we know we should do and what we end up doing. Paul said it this way, "I know that nothing good lives in me, that is, in my sinful nature. I have the desire to do good, but I cannot carry it out. For what I do is not the good I want to do; no, the evil I do not want to do—this I keep on doing" (Rom 7:18-19). Later on he sums up the experience by saying, "Wretched man that I am"(Rom 7:24). Whether we act against our conscience or someone who does so affects us, it feels awful and puts us face to face with one of our greatest problems.

What is your story of how God continues to help you with integrity? How could you work a gospel presentation into your story?

*Lack of meaning.* One of the most pervasive and tragic effects of our world system is superficiality. Victor Frankl, in his important book *Man's Search for Meaning,* says that seeking to find meaning in our lives is our greatest quest. He came to this conclusion as a young boy, and it proved true when he was a prisoner in Auschwitz. Most of what we are fed through advertisements and entertainment has little to do with establishing meaning in our lives. Henderson says it well: "If there is a point to our existence, I missed the announcement."[3]

This feeling of being lost contributes greatly to much modern angst. Haven't you felt this way? Wasn't this part of why you came to Christ? Or if you became a Christian as a child, isn't this why you still follow him? How could you mold your testimony to share with someone who experiences a significant lack of meaning?

*Low self-esteem.* Am I worthwhile? Does my life have value? Is there anything about me that is unique? While we all ask these questions at some point, some people are plagued by them every day. This insecurity is awful. It's a black cloud overshadowing the lives of those who experience it. It wears them down. If you are fortunate to have someone admit to you that he or she feels this way, you have a door opened to share your story of how God has built self-esteem in your life.

To do this, you will have to scrutinize your experiences to discover when you have experienced low self-esteem and how God met you in that need. Even if you are still feeling it, that's part of your story and you're going on in spite of it. You are witnessing in spite of a black cloud that hangs over you. That's a more powerful testimony than presenting yourself as having it all together. You have an *incomplete* story, like all the rest of us.

**Uncertainty about the future.** Especially after the terrorist attack against the World Trade Center in September 2001, the threat of anthrax and other weapons of mass destruction, the whole world feels insecure about the future. What is going to happen to me? To my family? To my job? What will happen to me after I die?

As Christians we may be uncomfortable admitting that we worry about the future. Nevertheless, we can't eradicate worry from our lives because, after all, we are *human* beings. Your story is not about how you are free from even the slightest temptation to worry. It centers on God and what he means to you in the face of uncertainties.

What is your ongoing story about how God helps you with uncertainty?

**God's apparent absence.** For many, God is absent from personal experience. The universe may be on their side, but an involved, caring God couldn't be. It's simply inconceivable.

What's your story about God being present? How did you become convinced that God is personal, that he's with you and for you? When, even as a Christian, have you felt like God was absent? How did God meet you in that difficult place? How can the gospel fit into that part of your story?

These modern problems color the lives of people today, Christian and non-Christians alike. One Christian friend of mine is going through a disappointment with his son. God seems disturbingly absent right now. As the Lord takes him through this, he will have a convincing testimony to share with unbelieving friends who feel an absence of God in their lives.

Outside of eternity the most important thing you possess may well be the story of how God works in your life. This is your credential. This is your authority to speak of Christ to anyone. Think of it this way: everything about your life has the possibility for bringing redemptive power to someone else. So although your story belongs to you, in a larger sense it belongs to God and resides as part of a large mosaic that includes the experiences of all believers from the beginning of time. What may presently remain a dim account in your mind may some day shine with particular relevance to the individuals that God, in his sovereignty, places within your sphere of influence.

We are obligated to practice introspection for the purpose of being prepared. Telling of God's story in our lives requires a transparency, openness and vulnerability that takes courage. It means that we must be honest about the sins done to us by other people, the sins we have committed and the sins that tempt us even now.

Our sin reminds us that we are still human, still in need of God's grace. Knowing this, we can be gracious to others caught in the fallen, human web. Evangelism is one sinner telling God's story to another. It is a horizontal, level exchange.

## JOSH'S STORY

Josh and I met when my husband and I were shopping for a new car. Josh is one of those happy people who seem to have an idyllic life. He and his wife are devoted to their children. Their young family is fun-loving and respecting of the needs of people around them. They're pleasant to be with and easy to love. After my aneurysm they wanted to help in any way they could, so one day I called Josh for a favor. When he arrived to pick me up, he put C. S. Lewis's *Mere Christianity* in my hand. He asked me if I had ever read it. "Yes, a long time ago," I replied. "Would you just glance at it, and tell me what you think of it now?" he asked. "I'm curious about what you think."

It took no longer than five minutes to get to my destination. While I waited for my appointment, I began to read the book and had enough time to peruse its general outline. I kept on reading while standing on the corner, waiting for Josh to pick me up. As I greeted him at the curb, I acknowledged the depth of the book's subject matter and asked for his impression of the book. He relayed that he found the message insightful, but disturbing. Parts of it rang true, but he just didn't think he had what it took to be a "real" Christian. He concluded that he couldn't be a Christian because he didn't "have what it takes to be *that* committed to Christ." Josh's problem seemed to be a crisis of integrity: he wasn't doing what he knew he needed to do and he was unwilling to change.

By now we were almost home, but Josh had just given me a marvelous opportunity, and I wanted to seize it. Mine was an opportunity much like Paul's with Agrippa. Neither Paul nor I knew many details about our audience's spiritual background. Though Josh and I talked frequently, up to this point my witness to him was primarily through attitude. I suspected the book had made him curious about spiritual things. Now he had opened the door for me to share the gospel. "Josh, I have some good news for you," I said. I went on to say that I'd love to tell him my story but it would require three to four minutes. I asked him if this was something he would like to hear now. He said he would.

So I cast my message to meet his immediate need. I explained that by our own nature, we all have unwilling hearts. Then I told my story, emphasizing how unwilling my heart was to forgive my parents and the mess I made of my life because of that. I explained that sin had created this situation. I briefly told him a couple of things my parents had done that made forgiveness humanly difficult for me. Then I emphasized what Jesus had done in dying on the cross and rising from the dead. I went on to share that he was alive right now. I spoke my version of Paul's words, "To this day I have had help from God," explaining that the Christian life is one where Jesus helps us do what we cannot do in our own strength—like have a willing heart to follow him.

All this took only a few minutes, and I wasn't rushed. Using Paul as a model, I gave him the gospel woven throughout my story. This gave him the freedom to ask more questions later, whenever he is so inclined. I was trying to stay within the time frame of three to four minutes.

Josh's life seems to be running smoothly. At this point he feels no "need" for God. I think I'm one of the first fishermen to pull on his net. When he's ready for talk of God, when he opens the door, God will put someone there to walk in. I hope it's me, but it could well be you.

Be ready with your stories. You never know when God will surprise you with an opportunity to share them.

---

## ENGAGE IN BECOMING INSIGHTFUL

---

1. What strikes you as important in this chapter?

2. I spoke early in the chapter about Bill, whose biggest challenge in becoming insightful was that he thought there was nothing noteworthy in his story. Can you identify some theological reasons for valuing our stories?

3. For each of the seven common, contemporary felt needs for the gospel, jot down a time in your life when God met this need in you.

   a. Alienation from others.

   b. Bad and unfair experiences.

   c. Conflict of integrity.

   d. Lack of meaning.

   e. Low self-esteem.

   f. Uncertainty about the future.

   g. God seemingly absent.

4. Read Acts 26:24-32, which concludes Paul's interview with Agrippa.

a. Describe how Paul brought his opportunity with Agrippa to a close.

b. Why is offering someone an opportunity to become a Christian an appropriate way to end a gospel presentation?

c. How would you determine whether it was appropriate to do this in any given situation?

# 11
# HOSPITABLE

## PUTTING ON AN
## EMERGENCY-ROOM ATTITUDE

*Turning around, Jesus saw them [two of John's disciples]*
*following and asked, "What do you want?"*

*They said, "Rabbi" (which means Teacher), "where are you staying?"*

*"Come," he replied, "and you will see."*

*So they went and saw where he was staying,*
*and spent that day with him.*

JOHN 1:38-39

**HOSPITALITY** involves several qualities: being interested in people, being receptive to having
guests, being generous and being fond of people,
especially strangers. Hospitality is essential in
evangelism where—when we hope to persuade
our unbelieving friends to come to Jesus—no action speaks louder to our friends than being invited into our home.

When I was growing up, our house was not open to visitors. It was dark and dirty, though not from dirt floors or lack of windows. My parents seemed uninterested in other people. Drawn drapes protected hung-over eyes and signaled opposition to any who may dare drop by. We were not encouraged to invite our friends over, and I don't recall ever having company. Even holiday dinners, hosted by either my grandmother or my aunt, were attended only by relatives. Those affairs were resisted by my parents and accompanied by tension. I have only one childhood memory of hospitality.

I was a teenager with my first boyfriend. I met Jim at music camp. He drove one hundred twenty-five miles to see me. Aunt Ellen invited Jim and me over for dinner. She fixed a feast of shrimp cocktail, roast beef, scalloped potatoes and more. I remember thinking that this must be the way normal people lived. I also knew at that moment that Aunt Ellen loved me enough to go through this extra effort.

So with this one positive memory buried inside, I slid into the Christian life without a clue about God's calling us to hospitality. I was, however, prepared to learn because as soon as Jesus came into my life, the whole world and all the people in it suddenly came to life for me. I was always interested in people, but now that interest took on new purpose. I wanted to know their stories. I wanted to know what they knew about God. Above everything else I wanted to treat others to what God was giving me through my new Christian friends. The natural consequence of this was that I began inviting people to our home, which is the essence of hospitality.

## HOSPITALITY MADE SIMPLE

Peter exhorts us to "offer hospitality to one another without grumbling" (1 Pet 4:9). First, Peter speaks of showing hospitality to one another, to friends who are already in the body of Christ. Second, he speaks of showing hospitality to strangers. Consider Hebrews 13:2, "Do not forget to entertain strangers, for by so doing some people have entertained angels without knowing it."

Not long ago I met a woman at church and, somehow, we found ourselves talking about hospitality. "I ought to take a class in it," she said as though it was a mystery, something difficult she needed to figure out. Since it is nearly a vanished art, I'd like to take time to dispense with the mystery and difficulty by boiling it down to its essence: to be hospitable is to exude a characteristic of God that involves two things—initiation and fondness. Christ has demonstrated both of these to us. He was once a stranger to us. Yet he initiated a relationship with us because he loved us. He did this through some means of witness, usually a Christian whose attitude and words we trusted.

Now we, too, represent his hands and his heart, and he desires that we be godly, hospitable ambassadors for people who are alienated from, and even fearful of, one another. God calls us to show people they are loved. What could speak more clearly of this than hospitality? Sometimes this means inviting a friend from work out to lunch or dinner. Other times it means asking someone to meet you at a coffee shop. It could even involve offering a glass of water to a solicitor at your door. God especially wants us to open the place where we live to friends and to strangers. I suspect that few things are more appealing to outsiders than the inside of our homes.

Everything I needed to know about being hospitable I learned from Lois the first evening she invited me to dinner in her home. She discovered Don was out of town and insisted I not be alone. When I arrived, she opened the door and warmly invited me in. I followed her to the kitchen where, to be frank, I expected to see the preparation of an elaborate meal. Lois's husband was a doctor and, to be perfectly honest, that raised my expectations. I saw nothing. I smelled nothing. As I began to wonder about this meal, she opened the refrigerator door and casually asked, "Let's see, what shall we have for dinner?" She wasn't kidding! Before long I had joined her search for food and her creative approach to preparation. Then we began cooking it together. Inwardly I breathed a big sigh of relief. *Even I can do this*, I thought.

After experiencing this comfortable approach (and the delicious result), not only did I know I could do this, but my heart desired to do it. When our hospitality emphasizes pleasing people rather than elaborately preparing for them, much of the stress evaporates. After a bit of practice, whether the occasion is spontaneous or planned, you will thoroughly enjoy hosting friends and strangers.

Not long after that evening, Lois wrote an article on hospitality where she likened it to healing. The connection makes complete sense because *hospital* (and thus *hospitality*) comes from the same root word for *guest*.[1] In a good hospital we are treated as a guest rather than as an object. Ideally, we are received with kindness. The hospital staff looks after our needs with grace and care. In a good hospital we are connected with resources that give us hope and health, even in emergencies. Similarly, as a Christian witness we may find our homes being a hospital to unbelievers with inner hurts, even emergencies. We are the hospital staff for this hurting world.

## LEARNING FROM THE GOOD SAMARITAN

One time a student of the law asked Jesus, "What must I do to inherit eternal life?" Jesus referred to the law, and the student rightly stated the most important one: " 'Love the Lord your God with all your heart and with all your soul and with all your strength and with all your mind' and 'Love your neighbor as yourself.' " Jesus responded, "Do this and you will live" (Lk 10:25-28).

The student must have felt uncomfortable after Jesus' response, similar to the way I felt when Lois went to the refrigerator and asked, "What shall we have for dinner?" The student asked Jesus, "And who is my neighbor?" I might have responded similarly to such a weighty command. So to make sure his answer would not be easily forgotten, Jesus wrapped a lesson about hospitality into a story and, in a matter of a few minutes, removed forever the idea that obedience to God is a matter of knowing stuff about him. Obedience is acting as he would act toward others, friends or strangers, emergency or not.

> "A man was going down from Jerusalem to Jericho, when he fell into the hands of robbers. They stripped him of his clothes, beat him and went away, leaving him half dead. A priest happened to be going down the same road, and when he saw the man, he passed by on the other side. So too, a Levite, when he came to the place and saw him, passed by on the other side. But a Samaritan, as he traveled, came where the man was; and when he saw him, he took pity on him. He went to him and bandaged his wounds, pouring on oil and wine. Then he put the man on his own donkey, took him to an inn and took care of him. The next day he took out two silver coins and gave them to the innkeeper. 'Look after him,' he said, 'and when I return, I will reimburse you for any extra expense you may have.'
>
> "Which of these three do you think was a neighbor to the man who fell into the hands of robbers?"
>
> [The lawyer] replied, "The one who had mercy on him."
>
> Jesus told him, "Go and do likewise." (Lk 10:30-37)[2]

We dare not trivialize what is communicated in the story of the Good Samaritan. Remember, Jesus tells this parable in response to the question, "What must I do to inherit eternal life?" It would be incorrect to suggest that one's salvation depends on one's being hospitable. Salvation depends on being in a trusting relationship with Jesus, as other Scriptures emphasize. But the gospel includes the truth that in relationship with Jesus, one is given the spiritual power and mandate to truly love God and neighbor. This love is expected to overflow into hospitality—even hospitality of the emergency-room sort Jesus describes here. God yearns for us to demonstrate this characteristic of his.

We can assume from the Samaritan's behavior that, had he not been traveling, he would have cared for this man in his own home. He was a mobile emergency room. He was in a dangerous place for a Samaritan—on the road between Jerusalem and Jericho. This road was notorious for robberies, and as a Samaritan he was a candidate for racial hatred and accompanying abuse. He was prepared with the ancient medicines of oil and wine, and he responded with empathy and mercy.

I have been told that not long ago on the campus of an American seminary, an unsettling experiment took place during finals week. On a narrow walkway between buildings the experimenters placed a man who appeared injured and untended. He may have looked much like the man the good Samaritan helped. He was lying down, unable to walk. Students swarmed by the man, rushing to take their next exam. Some saw the injured man. Others were too preoccupied to notice. Only one student stopped to help the injured man. As it turns out, his exams were completed and he felt he had the time to help.

In that place, where men and women are training to reach the world for Jesus, it is as if "in his name" they walk right by the very need Jesus commands us to attend. This experiment supports the unfortunate fact that even the most spiritually focused among us have learned to use a measure of priority that Jesus did not know. Jesus prioritized compassion. People who see themselves as a walking emergency room have the focus to shift their priorities when needs arise. Being hospitable requires a hefty dose of intentionality.

## PRIORITY SHIFT

Peter tells us to practice hospitality without complaining (1 Pet 4:9). Apparently I'm not the only one who sometimes starts my preparation for guests by reciting a litany of complaints. It's embarrassing to admit, especially since I know full well how faithful God is to me even at my weakest times and how thoroughly he gives me joy through hospitality. It's as if I step into an eternal dimension when I invite guests in. God honors hospitality. In fact, through our ministry of hospitality we may more frequently experience an unexpected presence, a divine presence, perhaps an angelic presence (Gen 18:1-22; Heb 13:2).

A couple of years ago I was given the opportunity to introduce my friend and housekeeper, Josefa, to Christ. Josefa turned her life over to Jesus that day. Now she attends church regularly.

One busy morning God invited me to shift my own priorities. Josefa was dusting the blinds in my family room when she turned to me and started talking about a bitter disappointment. She began to weep. I recognized the choice before me: I could nod in sympathy while excusing myself to attend a pressing editorial deadline, or I could take on the role of emergency-room staff. I chose the latter. (Thank goodness for that choice, since the pressing deadline was for this very chapter!) At that moment Josefa became a guest rather than a worker in my home.

We talked through her painful situation. We prayed together. I did what I could to encourage her. She went on to share that while she knew her family in Mexico loved her, she felt her Christian friends in the United States loved her even more. Our conversation took an hour out of my day, but you know what? As I went back to work, I heard her singing as she cleaned. I knew I had partnered with God in something far more important than writing this page.

Hospitality pushes us to new levels of faith. Our hospitality gives God the opportunity to show his love in practical ways to people who need it.

### IN CONSIDERATION OF STRANGERS

I remember reading a textbook on social psychology that described how "violence sells" in America. It assaults our movies, the fashion and demeanor of our youth, our casual language, our publications and our nightly news. Our fascination with violence has developed because the majority of us want to see it. It thrills and it sells. The consequence of being overexposed to violence is that it incubates a fear of living freely in the world—and this is a serious issue for Christians who set their focus on becoming hospitable to strangers. We're afraid the strangers among us may, indeed, be capable of horrendous crimes. So we limit contact with others and build social ghettos. Our homes become exclusively private. We even use security systems to protect ourselves from strangers. Of course, the reality is that most people are neither violent nor victims of violent crimes. The world is a friendlier place than we are led to believe.

Think of what the world would be like today if Jesus and his disciples had not practiced hospitality. If Jesus hadn't been fond of strangers—the poor, dispossessed, illiterate and inexperienced—he would have stayed in Nazareth and there would have been precious few converts. If the apostles hadn't been hospitable, they wouldn't have dared proclaim the good news. They wouldn't have had the motivation to take any of the risks involved in evangelism and building the church. Paul exuded a hospitable attitude even in the face of many dangers. When we read his epistles, we must remember that the nascent churches to which he was writing existed because Paul wasn't afraid of strangers. In Athens, where he very much hoped to connect with his audience, Paul instead received scorn and indifference. Still, he practiced hospitality; and because he did, churches sprang up in Europe and Asia. For Paul and the rest of the early Christians, being hospitable was as natural to their faith as praying.

### GUIDELINES FOR PRACTICING HOSPITALITY

What if we were to take the command to practice hospitality seriously? Here are a few simple guidelines to help make hospitality less overwhelming.

*Develop a hospitable attitude.* You may not be able to practice hospitality in your home for various reasons. Let that go. Don't allow that to keep you from being friendly or from initiating opportunities to develop friendships with others, especially strangers. Because of time constraints I've faced while writing this book, I've practiced hospitality more in cafés and coffee shops than at home, but I've enjoyed it just as much.

If you are having guests to your house, save the serious housecleaning for afterward, when you'll probably need it more! I know you probably didn't learn it in that order, but being hospitable isn't about perfection. Keep your home in functional order so that you'll never be embarrassed to spontaneously invite someone in.

My relationship with one of my most significant friends, who is committed to another religion, developed first through business. The first morning she dropped something off at my house, I had just returned home from working out. What I wanted most when the doorbell rang was a long, hot shower. It was my day to clean house, and there was a predictable mess. I answered the door. I invited her in and simply asked her to excuse the mess as I reached for the coffee. As I remember it, I only had a half cup of cold, stale coffee left, and she didn't have time for me to make a fresh pot. I simply stuck it in the microwave. Most important, though, we began a rewarding, deep relationship that day. I hope that one day I'll be sharing heaven with her.

*Avoid the "my home must be perfect before" syndrome.* Think dirt floors, dark rooms and a barnyard entry. You may be tempted to wait until the carpet is replaced or the flowers are planted, but even when those projects are finished, I bet you'll find another imperfection to keep you from being hospitable. Learn to use what you have rather than longing for more. We've always been a single-salary family, and I remember the years when Don's paycheck was financing three college educations. When our carpet was finally replaced, the installer humorously remarked that he hadn't seen that kind of padding in years. Countless times before company came I prayed that they just wouldn't see the permanent spots on the rug (or that if they did, I wouldn't notice their response). Every time we had company, I found myself first jumping over the "my home must be perfect" hurdle.

*Practice hospitality as you can, not as you cannot.* If you're not a gourmet cook, don't set yourself up to fail as one—unless, of course, you've always wanted to improve your cooking and intentional hospitality can be your motivation to try. If you are a gourmet cook, make sure you allow joy and conversation and relaxation to pervade your preparation time. My advice for you perfectionists is to not let your standards be so high that your guests are too intimidated to reciprocate your hospitality.

I remember the evening when Lois's husband, Larry, came to our house for dinner and we were having such a stimulating conversation that I let the creamed soup boil. The soup was ruined in terms of presentation and we didn't have time to start over. What was Larry's response? He blithely assured me that the nutrients were still in place. We kept up the lively conversation, ate curdled soup and still chuckle at the memory. The important thing I've learned is that our guests are usually grateful to have any meal at all with us in our home.

*Get as much help as you need.* Whether it's a spur-of-the-moment lunch or a dessert party, your guests will often offer to bring food. Let them. I have a friend with a busy schedule who was having her son's college basketball team over for dinner. Logically there were many reasons not to do this. But she got help. She called her son's favorite Italian restaurant and ordered enough lasagna for the whole team; her priority was to provide a relaxed atmosphere where she could get to know his friends. If you can afford such a luxury, enjoy it!

The following story illustrates how easy hospitality can be when it's kept simple.

### LIZA'S STORY

I went into the ophthalmologist for my annual eye exam. At the time, I was reading *Moby Dick,* arguably the most challenging book I've ever read. That said, I was lost in another world when Liza came to the waiting room and called out my name. She was going to give me an initial exam. First, she asked me what I was reading. When I answered her question, I explained how difficult this book was to read. Liza told me that she loves to read and that she yearns to read good literature. She added that with working full time and caring for her toddler, she just didn't have much time to do so. I sensed that she was grappling with wanting to do things she didn't have time for. As the conversation continued, she asked what I did professionally.

I told her that, in addition to being a teacher, I was a writer and that my main work is adult studies on character development from a spiritual perspective. Intrigued, I suppose, her questions continued. It was evident from how she framed her questions that she was very intelligent. I explained to her that I was a Christian and that the studies I wrote were biblically based. Liza revealed her desire to know more about the Bible. Raised in a formal, liturgical church, she had little intimate knowledge of Scripture and had many unanswered questions. It appeared that Liza was just waiting for a Christian to come into her life to help her sort things out from a spiritual perspective.

As we talked during the preliminary exam, two things became clear: Liza was both spiritually open and desiring to grow. I shared these observations, which surprised her. She wasn't accustomed to hearing this kind of affirmation. Her spirits were obviously lifted. It was also clear that Liza liked talking to me, and by now you know that's one of my criteria for proceeding further. When someone likes you, it's a good and reliable indication that God has prepared this person to receive what you have to say. I hadn't slipped into this conversation with any ulterior motive; I simply started answering her questions about what I was reading.

I quickly discovered that Liza was a delightful person—and I know that I tend to think nearly everyone is because, in truth, nearly everyone is! I enjoyed our conversation. Given this experience, I decided to see just how interested Liza was in pursuing the spiritual issues in our conversation. I told her I lived close by and invited to her to come to my home for lunch sometime so she could share her religious questions with me. Liza accepted my invitation. Her parting comment to me gave me the insight I needed to schedule it. Wistfully she asked, "You won't forget me, will you?"

My insight was that in her last comment, Liza was inviting me to move quickly. In honesty, I admit that when I'm writing, I don't like to stop for an actual meal. I take a quick break, walk from the desk to the kitchen and back again with a plate of food. I must break this routine when God has obviously handed me an invitation to serve him through hospitality.

Consider again the unusual context of our meeting. Liza was at work where she was the professional and I was the patient. Also, Liza is a young Hispanic woman, and it's unusual for someone like her to be that transparent with someone like me, a white woman old enough to be her mother and reading intimidating classical books. Culturally this was an unusual situation for both of us. Liza was spiritually hungry and I was offering her soul food. It seemed that Liza was dealing with issues of meaning and bad or unfair experiences. How did I know this from my brief experience with her in the doctor's office? The only answer I can give is that we gain insight from experience. Little clues she gave me initially (her interest in reading significant literature, an overall sadness that I sensed in her) led me to these conclusions. I just knew there was unresolved pain underneath her professional exterior.

When Liza arrived for lunch a week later, she wanted to immediately start a dialogue about spiritual things. She wanted me to talk about why I was a Christian. So I told my gospel story. I quickly told her about how some painful and unfair childhood experiences had created in me a hunger for meaning and how Jesus had met me at that point of need. Liza was moved enough by my story to begin her own.

What she was feeling above all else was a desire to be attached meaningfully to God. As a Christian, I knew that she felt alienated from God, but I couldn't bring myself to say this directly because I feared it would only intensify the feeling. What I could say was, "Liza, obviously, you are searching for God and you want life to have meaning. Does my story make sense to you? Do you see how God could help you?" Liza readily affirmed she could.

"Would you like to pray right now for Jesus to come into your life?" I had prepared her for this question by using these words in my testimony. Slowly and hesitantly Liza replied, "I need to think more about this. I don't want to be rushed and I really have to get back to work now."

You can see that if I had asked her beforehand just how much time we would have together, I would have changed my approach. I assured her she could have all the time she needed, and I told her to call me when she wanted to talk further. I give Liza colossal credit for coming that day. Think about your life before you became a Christian. Would you have gone to the home of a stranger to talk about your spiritual issues? I decided that if she didn't call me within a month, I would call her and set up another lunch, if she wanted.

Life interfered. Within a couple of weeks I was having brain surgery. The chances of a quick recovery, any recovery really, were slim to none. I spent a month of my life in the hospital. I was also unable to drive for several more months and wasn't physically up to seeing many people.

But the aneurysm changed my vision, so when I could finally drive, one of my first excursions was to the ophthalmologist's office for a new lens prescription. I had prayed intermittently for Liza in the six months since seeing her, and I was hoping I would see her that day. I remember asking God to rekindle our budding friendship. Later, when Liza and I did meet again, I discovered that God was indeed doing just that. On the day before my visit, Liza said she had been thinking about me enough to mention me to her husband. So when she saw my name on the patient roster, she had a big smile on her face.

When she found out about my illness, she expressed alarm. Her concern for me was touching and I thanked her. I also told her the next chapter of my story. "I know it sounds horrible, Liza, and for many people an aneurysm like mine leads either to death or serious disability. But God has healed me. I won't permanently suffer, and I think I'm a better person for having gone through this. You don't need to feel sorry for me, but I would just love it if you would join me in giving thanks to God for what he has done."

I saw Liza struggle to grasp this, but she could see that I was sincere. When I invited her for lunch again, she agreed (and when she came, I made sure to ask her how much time we had to meet). She filled me in on the last six months of her life. She was still in much the same place, filled with the same longings and concerns. I simply listened. When it was time for her to return to work, I asked her if she would like to meet weekly on her lunch hour to keep talking about these issues. Liza made this commitment eagerly.

The next Tuesday we began. She came for lunch with her questions and concerns. Again, I just listened. All that she said led me to see that she was seriously eager for God, but she was on the outside, looking in and afraid to walk toward him. After a while I shared what I saw and asked her if she was ready to pray to have Jesus come to live inside her. I admitted that I did not know anything that would help her more. I explained that if Jesus were living inside of her, he would give her the resources to deal with her issues. I was honest in saying that it would take time, but that if she invited Jesus in today, she could leave my house knowing that she was beginning her journey with him. Again I shared the gospel, only this time I put her story into it. After hearing it that day, Liza was ready to take that step of faith, so I led her in a simple prayer. I began to pray and then asked her to follow my example. She was able to do this because she knew what to pray for.

I wish I could tell you that bells and whistles went off, that Liza's face glowed, that this was an extraordinary, observable conversion. Instead, it was quiet and simple. It was consistent with Liza's demeanor, which I find is most often the case. People respond to conversion in ways consistent with their personalities. Time has proved this conversion was authentic and real.

Shortly after this I went out of town for three months. I prayed for Liza and I was anxious to see how God was working in her life. When I called her after returning to town, we resumed our weekly lunches, and slowly she became more like a family member than a guest in our home. Sometimes I had no time to prepare lunch beforehand and, as I learned from Lois, I let her help me fix whatever we could find in the refrigerator. Eventually a program for new Christians began in our church. Liza and her husband responded to my invitation to come. Day by day Liza's spiritual story grows and unfolds, and I have the privilege of watching it.

Bringing Liza to Jesus was as natural as serving a meal to a hungry friend. But Liza faces obstacles to serving him as King in the fellowship of the church; she needs patience and the presence of compassionate Christians. Her family needs her income. She deals with chronic pain from a back injury, and she has emotional stress from events in her childhood not yet fully resolved. Time and financial pressures constitute her major hurdles. Frankly I don't know how she does all she does, considering what she juggles every day. I do know that I continue praying for her to find a creative way to serve Jesus as King within the fellowship of his church.

My primary contribution to her now is to provide all the encouragement I can. Her issues need to be addressed one at a time. We talk honestly about this when we meet for lunch. Liza takes tiny steps forward at a speed that she can handle. In the meantime there always seems to be enough food in my refrigerator, and it's a pleasure to share it with Liza—once a stranger, but now a dear friend.

---

### ENGAGE IN BECOMING HOSPITABLE

---

1. What information about hospitality in this chapter is helpful for you?

2. Examine your own practice of hospitality. On a scale of one to ten (with ten being highest), where would you put yourself on this hospitality scale? Why did you choose the number you did?

   a. How do your childhood experiences of hospitality influence your attitude toward it today?

   b. What encouraging things can Christians do today to develop the regular practice of hospitality with unbelievers?

3. Read the story of the good Samaritan in Luke 10:29-37.

a. Why do you think the priest and Levite ignored the injured man?

b. What reasons do people today give for not being hospitable?

c. What all did it cost the Samaritan to practice hospitality?

d. What speaks to you most clearly in this parable?

# 12

## CREATIVE

### THE POSSIBILITIES OF GREEN HAIR

*We should, to begin with, think that God leads*
*a very interesting life, and that he is full of joy.*

DALLAS WILLARD


*In the beginning was the Word, and the Word was with God,*
*and the Word was God. He was with God in the beginning.*

*Through him all things were made;*
*without him nothing was made that has been made.*
*In him was life, and that life was the light of men.*
*The light shines in the darkness,*
*but the darkness has not understood it.*

JOHN 1:1-5


**CREATIVITY** is the God-given ability to bring about something new, something that has never existed before. In evangelism it means to follow God's leadership in creating what is required for our unbelieving friends to have an *Aha!* experience with God.

A woman came to a Life Design study entitled "Fully Alive." She was a faithful church member, loyal to Christian beliefs and bored to death! She shared with her small-group leader that contrary to the study's title, she was "fully dead." Desperation can make us courageous. This woman was realizing that the fault was not in what she believed but in how she was living it.

When I first read Dallas Willard's assertion "that God leads a very interesting life,"[1] I went wild with hope. His statement confirmed a truth that I had been dancing around but had not taken seriously since childhood. In fact, in my childhood I was encouraged to not take it seriously.

I grew up in a farming community that was long on traditional values and patriotism and short on creativity. I grew up hearing a litany of observations from those I held most dear: "You have the *strangest ideas!*" they said, shaking their heads. "We don't do it *that* way; we do it like *this*," they warned. "You don't *really* want to do that." To their credit they thought they were doing me a favor. They were shaping me up for a predictable and acceptable life. They felt certain that once rehabilitated, freed from my strange view of life, I would fit in just fine.

The problem with this sort of caring resolve is that God did not create any of us to live exactly as anyone else does. Yes, he wants each of us to live out his teachings, but how we do this involves a unique blend of our gifts, talents, passions, personality and experience.

## Creativity as a Basic Ingredient in Evangelism

Thank God for buoyancy! When I moved from my rural hometown to Washington, D.C., I looked around and took a deep breath. I was in my element! The change transferred me from black-and-white to Technicolor. Washington brims with diversity. I didn't have to walk more than ten feet before I met someone with a different slant on life. Before I even knew him, God was issuing me an invitation to enjoy the world and the people he created.

He was also preparing me for a future as an evangelist. Washington was my schoolyard. It was my Investigation 101 course. I discovered the theater and concert halls. I visited museums during my lunch hour. The Corcoran Art Museum and the National Gallery of Art were both within walking distance of my office. I read the classics. Through this I experienced marvelous conversations with intriguing people, some of whom became good friends. Six years later when I became a Christian, the framework for how I would live was in place and ready to support a new structure.

The dimension of creativity that God gave me through the Holy Spirit proved essential in my becoming an effective evangelist. I'm not alone. In the most moving spiritual conversion stories I hear or read, God's creativity is profoundly present. True, some people simply ooze creativity; everything they touch or influence seems original, but creativity is more than native style. Whether we were given the freedom to be creative as a child or not, we who are made in the likeness of God can learn to see life and respond to it as he does—creatively. We can ask him for a creative approach to evangelism within the sphere of our natural talents and personality.

Creative evangelism is the God-given ability to bring about something new, something that has never been before, something that provides unbelievers with the *Aha!* experience of realizing truths about God they didn't know before. There is mystery and excitement here. I picture in my mind seven sculptors, each handed an identical lump of clay and told to make something useful for serving. We know that each sculptor works with precisely the same tools: two hands, two eyes and one mind. And, for goodness sake, each has the exact material available. But are their creations boring or predictable? On the contrary, the results cause the observer to marvel: seven distinctive styles, seven distinctive results—seven objects of beauty shaped by seven creative people. The molding of evangelistic method is equally unpredictable and exciting.

Watch out, because God is going for something new through you!

## THE ORIGINS OF CREATIVITY

God graces every life with creativity. In Scripture, creation is a work of initiation, of bringing forth something entirely new. Consider some of what our God has initiated. He created a vast universe with billions and billions of galaxies in a seemingly limitless space that still confounds us. He created whatever we are seeing when we look at things closer at hand—stars, rolling seas, snow-swept tundra, mountain peaks and wild flowers in remote, unexpected places. What does it mean that he creates animals and insects (close to a million species of insects, by the way) that share this planet but see it and use it in utterly different ways than we do? And who are we? Are we breathless over considering the uniqueness of our being as often as we should be? Are we excited that in all the people who lived before us and the six billion or so who share the Earth with us now, there are not and never have been duplicates? No wonder Willard is convinced that God's life is interesting!

But then came sin, the human tragedy that causes the entire Earth to suffer. God, though, brought something new: forgiveness is his creative solution that allows us to function in the ongoing presence of evil and pain. God is the all-powerful Creator and his power is linked to his creativity (Rom 1:20). Through this power, God creates new life in us. "Therefore, if anyone is in Christ, he is a new creation; the old has gone, the new has come" (2 Cor 5:17). One of the most powerful ways we can experience this new life is by living as forgiven people and telling our non-Christian friends about it. We know God's forgiveness by dealing with our own sins and the sins committed against us. No two of us have exactly the same story of redemption. God is initiating, through each of our unique lives, a creative story of forgiveness and a fresh way of telling it.

Human creativity is usually thought of in terms of the development of objects, from paintings to freeway systems. But when you look at the things God has initiated, a broader application fits. Think of the different life experiences and talents each person possesses. They shed light on the various facets of God's character and his creativity in ways we simply cannot know by observing only our own life.

Consider also how differing cultures (which are of God's making, according to Gen 11) reveal a part of God that we cannot grasp if we are focused entirely on our own view. I have learned far more about how to practice hospitality from my Arab friends than from my friends closer to home. I understand aspects of teamwork from the Japanese that I could not learn from my independent American colleagues.

Because God has an interesting life, we who are born of him should expect one as well. What is it, then, that causes us to live as though we are poor when our Father has handed us this great fortune? What causes us to ignore such wealth or hide it beneath the mattress? God loves each of us, whether we are uptight or cut-loose, organized or messy. We are objects of his love, and we are the means by which he reaches the world. We are surprised that there are as many approaches to telling the gospel story as there are people to share it with. In my experience of watching others engaged in evangelism, I find the greatest joy comes from seeing or hearing something I've not seen or heard before. Nothing seems to compare with the delight we have when we follow God's nudges to interact with people. When we are open to being creative, we think new thoughts and do things that we never imagined doing.

If telling the truth creatively is that wonderful, how do we begin to do it? It's simple but not easy. It's different from the approaches usually suggested in our Christian subculture. It may sound inconsistent, but to "let go" and become creative we must first become very quiet, inwardly quiet. To do this we must spend time alone with God. We must seek to develop all the characteristics in this book. As we cultivate these qualities, we find ourselves more dependent on God's direction, which can be heard only with a quiet heart. While the outer world powers up like the spin cycle of a washer, we learn to slow down and listen for God's voice inside us. In our inner quiet an ongoing dialogue takes place. It's a give-and-take conversation between us and our heavenly Father about all that is around us.

As you listen to God, you will begin to notice things like the way a waiter goes about his job. You'll be mesmerized watching a father holding his infant son and gazing on him with pure delight. You'll hear a comment on a television show that you can't forget, and then several days later you realize that this comment contributed to an evolving insight. There is certainly an element of mystery in this learned quiet; and in my experience evangelical Christians aren't accustomed to thinking of their lives as an unfolding mystery. We need to remember that in evangelism we aren't entirely in control: we don't know exactly how things will turn out, and we cannot orchestrate the placement of people along our path. We are in for plenty of God-surprises. And aren't we fundamentally happy about that? Life, as God intends it to be lived, is an adventure.

I once saw a Renoir painting where the artist had painted small portraits of a person in different stages of life. Take a few quiet moments now to think about the mystery that God, as the creative artist, is unfolding within and around you. Think about your experience of evangelizing as a canvas on which Jesus paints the scenes. The dominant theme in the painting is God's creativity. On my canvas I see the scene in which I have lunch with Liza and talk about things that I sense will create openness to God; there's a scene of me and James having dinner and starting our dialogue about spirituality. Our canvas will not be finished until our earthly lives are over.

It's a stretch, but let's suppose that in heaven there is a gallery showing an exhibition called "Creativity in Evangelism." Jesus is the featured artist, and he personally leads the tour through the gallery. We watch with delight as he tells the stories of each evangelist represented here. We who are obedient to the call of evangelism, who dare to take a creative approach to truth-telling, have been painted by Jesus as light in someone's darkness. He tells us about the creativity and symbolism of each painting. In this gallery there are no alarm systems, no stanchions and ropes to hold us back. We are allowed to *ooh* and *ah*, to touch and to marvel at the beauty and distinctions found in painting after painting. We linger at each piece because no two are the same; no reproductions found among the rooms of originals. How amazing this Jesus is, and how marvelous are these, his works.

## PHILLIP'S STORY

Attention to subtlety is not often among our strong points in this boisterous world, yet God often speaks to us through gentle nudges. One came to me when we parked our car across the street from a theater where a rock concert was about to begin. The long line of expectant concertgoers stretched down the street. Everyone looked to be between the ages of eighteen and twenty-three. They were dressed mostly in black. As I moved closer to the crowd, it hit me that I was completely out of touch with what people their age were thinking, what they valued, who they were listening to. Suddenly, unbidden, this thought came to me: *I wish I could go to this concert and experience what this group will soon experience. I wonder what they think and how they feel.* This was an unusual thought for me because I've never—not even as a teenager in the era of Chuck Berry and Elvis—enjoyed rock music. Nevertheless, I had a strong desire to be a fly on that theater wall.

Several days later I went to a restaurant highly recommended by a young friend. As I waited for my lunch, I noticed one of the waiters. His buzz-cut hair was dyed green, so you may not be surprised that I noticed him. But I noticed something else about him as well—something winsome in his steady and unhurried pace, his encouraging smile, his obvious focus on being helpful. At that moment my attention was arrested.

My friend was right: it was a fabulous restaurant. And it was near to the gym where I exercised, so the next week I went back there for lunch. The green-haired waiter was working again with the same marvelous smile. This time I engaged him in a short conversation. I found out his name was Phillip. I also discovered he was nineteen. Recalling my encounter at the theater only weeks prior, I wondered whether he would let me be a fly on his life's wall. On my next restaurant visit I asked if I could interview him. He kindly agreed, explaining he was available any day after work. I told him I would come up with a time during the following week.

Before I left I asked if he wondered why I wanted this interview. Offhandedly he asked me to tell him. I explained that I wanted to get into the mind of a nineteen-year-old person. I wanted to know what he thought and what was important to him. That prompted him to reply that in light of this, he'd like for me to interview him in his living space. He resided in a poor, unsafe part of town. I began to wonder if I wasn't biting off more than I could chew. Still, curiosity drove me to keep our appointment.

Going to his apartment was a risk, perhaps even a big one. To risk means to let go of what is known and reach out to something you're not sure of yet. That links it directly to creativity—the bringing forth of something new. There's no way to evangelize creatively without taking risks that are chosen with wisdom.

I did not feel threatened, really. It was after I told Phillip I wanted to understand his generation that he invited me to see how he lives. His was a generous invitation. I had also seen enough of him to sense he could be trusted. Nevertheless, I called my husband before I left and gave him the specifics.

The interview developed into one of the most joyful learning experiences of my life. I got to Phillip's small apartment, and it was neat as a pin. I met his gray-and-white cat, which acts like my dog (it was loving and friendly). This cat jumped on my lap and snuggled up to be petted. I was beginning to feel safe, and everything about his living space told me that I was in the presence of a creative and loving person. Bright, original art covered his walls. His cat acted friendlier than most, and I attributed this in part to Phillip's loving personality. Phillip began burning sage. I had never seen this done, and I really didn't know at first what he was doing, so I asked him. Casually he replied that he burned sage because it smelled good and would purify the room and cleanse it. "Does it bother you?" he asked, adding quickly that he would extinguish it if I preferred. His genuine, sensitive response put most of my concern to rest. Then he shared his story. As it unfolded, I realized that I was also in the presence of brilliance.

Phillip grew up with a drug-abusing, paranoid schizophrenic mother. Having no contact with extended family or other responsible adults, his mother lacked accountability. She viewed each of her four children as unwanted burdens and nuisances. When she wasn't partying, she spent most of her time in bed. His memories were filled with his mother's parties where the drugs and alcohol flowed freely. I shuddered to think of what Phillip was exposed to. His mother didn't allow her children to play outside and she didn't believe in school, so regardless of state law, Phillip was never enrolled—not in grade school, not in junior high, not in high school. Despite such circumstances of internal and external darkness, Phillip had taught himself to read by the age of four. Using everything he could find, he became extraordinarily creative.

At seventeen Phillip walked away from the terrors of his family and into the terrors of the streets for a year. Then he briefly lived with an older sister. He landed his first job bussing tables at a café where he earned enough money to share an apartment with one of his friends.

I was struck with this story. In the first place, much of it paralleled my own. If we hadn't lived in a small town and if my grandmother hadn't lived across the street, occasionally rescuing me and my siblings from the abuses of our alcoholic parents, I don't know that my mother would have put any of us in school. In my teen years my mother also was afflicted with paranoid schizophrenia and spent time in mental hospitals. But, unlike with Phillip, the effect all this had on me was to make me angry, not kind. I was dumbfounded by his lack of bitterness. Finally I asked him why had he not become a drug abuser? Why was he not bitter?

"Well, this may sound strange, but I feel like I've been shrouded by the grace of God all my life. I've seen horrible things, I've experienced awful stuff but somehow God has just taken me through it. I'm blessed," he said. It turned out that several times he was briefly placed in foster homes and on some of those occasions, his foster parents were Christians.

Then I commented on his apparent lack of bitterness toward his mother. "I just don't want to be bitter. I don't want to live like her— she seems to hate everything and everybody. I go back to visit her just to remind myself of what I don't want to be." I was nowhere near such maturity when I was Phillip's age, and I certainly had no acquaintance with such wisdom. His story was so nearly unbelievable that I carefully asked, "Phillip, this story is so unusual, why should I believe you?"

He was quiet for a moment. Then he reached up to pet his cat, who was sleeping on the back ledge of his chair. With a kind smile and a quiet voice he said, "You don't have to believe me, Chris." He offered to take me to his mother's house.

When I asked if he wanted to go to school, I saw his passion. "I want to go to school more than anything! I just don't know where to go, how to get started."

Every time I saw Phillip it was after a workout. I was in old workout clothes and covered with sweat; my hair was disheveled and I wore no makeup. I'd drag my weary body into his restaurant for a quick lunch and say hello. So I said, laughing: "Phillip, I know I don't much look like it, but I am well-connected. I'm going to call around and find a way for you to go to school. I'll give you the information, and you will have to take it from there." He was thrilled. And all I could think of was how happy I was that I had acted on this hunch to interview him. I didn't yet know the extent of his Christian involvement, but it was obvious God was an important and real part of his life already. I did get in touch with someone who could place Phillip according to his skills and needs. He gathered his courage, enrolled immediately and embarked on his journey.

Words seem so flat now, in this attempt of mine to describe my joy in meeting with Phillip. But I had the distinct impression that God was at work in his life and that he was inviting me to be his partner in creatively sharing love and encouragement with this young man. As I drove away from his little apartment toward the safety of my own home, I hadn't words or heart enough to thank God for enriching my life through this opportunity to help Phillip.

Think for a moment what it might be like to have been brought up as he was. His memories of childhood are mostly dark. The bright spots centered on creative projects, like designing paper houses and making sculptures out of Christmas cards "old church ladies" had passed on to him. Here he is today trying to make his own way. He doesn't know how to drive. He walks to and from work. He's basically alone. He has no health-care benefits, no cushion for any kind of emergency. He can't go to his mother for any financial support; and his father, who has never shown an interest in him, has been out of the picture for years. How would you feel if you were in his situation?

In our second interview I focused my questions on Phillip's family and his experience with discipline. Then we talked about what it meant to live in a healthy family, and how he would need that kind of support to get through school. I mentioned that he would have to learn to drive and that it was important for him to find health care. Finally I said, "Phillip, I'm certain God has a special vocation for you. The problem is that because you're so creative, you could get sidetracked by lesser things. You have a natural ability to work with people. You have an extensive vocabulary, and you have keen intelligence. Right now, you're an open slate. What if, through your studies and exposure to academic disciplines, you realize you want to go to college, maybe even head for graduate school? You certainly have the capacity for it."

"Do you really think God has something special for me to do, Chris?" he asked, his head bowed, his voice quiet and wavering. With all the tenderness and strength I could muster, I responded,

"Yes, Phillip. I'm certain of it."

"Sometimes I feel so *stupid*. There are so many things I just don't know about. So many things I just don't know how to do. Are you certain that God has something special in mind for me?"

Then I asked him if I could share a couple of my own stories about not knowing how to do basic things. He wanted to hear them. Children who grow up without participating parents don't learn basic living skills. I simply didn't know how to make a bed that wouldn't come apart in the middle of the night. Even though Don never remarked about it, I knew that there had to be a more substantial way to make a bed. Finally I got tired of remaking the bed everyday, so, in tears, I called Carol and asked if she would come over and teach me how to do it. I can't convey how stupid and vulnerable I felt. Carol knew how difficult it was for me to make this call. She assured me that she'd be right over. When she came, we started at the beginning. She explained it all, she showed me how, and she coached me as I did it. Our bed hasn't come apart since that lesson! Never in a thousand years did I think making beds would be a vital part of my gospel story. But God is so creative!

Phillip's smile was my reward for sharing something that was ultimately private to me and helpful to him. I went on. "One evening a group of friends was playing Pictionary. I got the word *forearm*. I knew this was a simple word and that everybody else knew it, but I was stuck. Finally I slipped out of the room with my trusted friend, Elli. I explained my predicament, and she insisted that it was natural with my background that I would not know about forearms. Then she raised my arm and pointed to my forearm. Again, I felt so stupid. But the reality was that in my primary school years my mother was drunk early in the morning and unable to communicate; when she was sober, she was largely disinterested. Are these the kind of things you mean when you say you feel stupid, Phillip?" I asked. He nodded quietly.

When these two experiences happened to me, I never thought they might be useful to someone else. I just tucked them away mentally in my memory file, in the "special memories of friendship" folder, not in the "special memories of stupidity" folder. When I needed those memories, God brought them to mind. He creatively used them to show Phillip that his experience of feeling stupid was understandable and natural. I'm certain God doesn't want either of us to remain stuck in feelings of inferiority.

Before ending that conversation I wanted to open our dialogue about spirituality. I hope this is an ongoing dialogue between us, one that never ends. I could have assumed that Phillip was a Christian. After all, a feeling of being shrouded by the grace of God *sounds* Christian. A Bible in Phillip's small living room *looks* Christian. He *acted* Christian when I prayed for him after our first interview. A song he wrote and sent to me about God could be sung in my church. Still, a prudent evangelist does not make assumptions. So in this second interview I asked whether he considered himself a Christian.

Looking me straight in the eye, he reluctantly replied, "No, because I can't be like some of the Christians I know." Then he went on to tell me the story of getting involved in an "awesome" church. He had fallen in love with one of the girls in the youth group. "We had a pure relationship, Chris, but some women in the church thought something was going on, and they took it upon themselves to judge me. And that wasn't all. My hair really looked cool then. It was dyed yellow, orange and red, and I had it in dreadlocks. These Christian women told me that I was supposed to be a representative of Jesus and I couldn't be that while I looked like this. I decided then that I couldn't be a Christian. I didn't want to become judgmental like them."

Surely those Christian women didn't intend to crush Phillip's spirit. I wonder whether they knew his background or whether they had ever really listened to any of his story. What if they had prayed for the creativity to love Phillip in ways that would draw him to Jesus? Today the organized church has largely lost the audience of Phillip's generation. It's time for us to ask some hard questions. What has our unimaginative behavior cost the church? Do our current attitudes and behaviors reflect cultural or biblical Christianity?

You may get a chance to meet Phillip because he left Ventura, California. By now he might be in your town. Perhaps he's added tattoos or body piercings. He may have rings hanging from his nose and eyebrows. The last time I heard from him was an e-mail message sent from Berkeley. He's living on the street again, without a job and without an education. I don't know whether there was more I could have done to be a more substantial friend. God allowed the meshing of common experiences and feelings to be shared for a time between us. The path Phillip is taking has not yet led to the kingdom.

When I received news from him of his whereabouts, I immediately contacted a Christian friend in the Berkeley area who was willing to help do whatever it took to help Phillip be self-sufficient and get connected to a Christian support system. Then I sent Phillip an e-mail telling him the support was available if he wanted it. Thus far he hasn't responded.

My gut tells me that Phillip can't yet receive the kind of loving support he needs from anyone. His former employer told me that he had never met anyone who felt so bad about himself. Only God can bring the next Christian into his life. In the meantime I pray for him. And I especially pray that creativity will be lavished upon the next believer God puts on his path.

## AND THEN WHAT?

What do we do when what we did didn't seem to work? We seek from God the strength to not abandon the challenge before us. We keep on keeping on. We recognize that we are not the Savior, we only follow him. We go where he goes, and he said he goes to seek the lost.

Recently I met another peer of Phillip's, and I was again struck by how much the church needs to rethink its approach to this generation. This young woman's name is Christina. I commented that we had nearly the same name and asked her whether she knew what our name meant. "I think it has something to do with Christ, but I'm not sure," she replied nonchalantly.

"You're right. It means follower of Christ," I said. "I think that's a wonderful thing to be named for. What do you think?"

"Yuck," she spurted out. "I don't want to be known as a Christian. I don't want to have anything to do with organized religion," she concluded.

It is time the organized church takes the kind of risks necessary to creatively spread God's love and encouragement to Phillip's generation. He tells me that he has many friends who have no parental support, who really need an "adult sponsor." The stakes have never been higher.

## ENGAGE IN BECOMING CREATIVE

1. What did you learn about creativity in this chapter?

2. What do you think lies behind the fact that Jesus took part in creation? What do you think it means that *you* are part of his creation?

3. Complete this sentence, "When I think about being creative in evangelism, I . . ."

4. Read about Lydia's conversion to Christianity in Acts 16:13-15.

   a. This is the first recorded conversion on the continent of Europe. How does this text reflect creativity as it is described in this chapter?

   b. As a Jewish man, Paul was familiar with the daily prayer, "Thank God I am not a woman." What might Paul have felt when he discovered that the only people worshiping God on that sabbath were women? How does his behavior reflect creativity?

   c. Later, a church meets in Lydia's home, in Europe (see Acts

16:40). Today many masterpieces of art in the great museums of Europe have a biblical theme. What would have been lost if Paul had not taken this God-given opportunity with Lydia?

d. What application does this story have for you with the people you are evangelizing? What is one thing you could do this week because of it?

# 13
# CONSISTENT

## WHEN STRAWBERRIES
## AREN'T ENOUGH

*None of us should listen to a man giving a lecture
or a sermon on his "philosophy of life"
until we know exactly how he treats his wife, his children,
his neighbors, his friends, his subordinates—and his enemies.*

SIDNEY J. HARRIS

*"My food," said Jesus, "is to do the will of him
who sent me and to finish his work."*

JOHN 4:34

CONSISTENT is a quality marked by harmony and steady continuity. To be consistent in evangelism means behaving as Jesus would in each relationship with non-Christian friends while remaining true to our God-given call to fulfill the Great Commission. We are helped in developing consistency when we apply the New Testament "one another" commands for relationships.

If consistency were a person, her personal story might read like this: "Long ago, before the world began I existed to represent all that stands firm. Mine was an *unimpaired condition*. I haven't changed, even though I recognize that many Christians today have limited their understanding of me to certain beliefs. But I can't be confined here. If you will, visualize me as a colorful beach ball by the seashore, in the hands of Buoyant. One of my colorful stripes is friendliness. Acceptance is another. Honor is another. I could go on about my stripes, but you get the idea.

"I am a quality that has survived countless trends in evangelism. I don't mind the trends, as long as they remain biblical. Cultural awareness may well encourage a redesign of one's approach to gospel truth, but I do not change. I'm extending to you an invitation to become my close friend. I will come alongside to assist you in evangelism. I don't mean to make you uncomfortable, but I will attend you, diligently; I will point out those personal characteristics you need to live in harmony with the biblical commands for relationships. I want to see you stand as sturdy and as delightfully as a field of corn. Think of me as *complete* and *undivided*, for this is what I am like and this is what you will become if you cultivate my friendship."

When I think of Consistency, this is how I imagine her.

## CONSISTENCY STEPS IN

Consistency is the stuff of staying power: intentional, firm, filled with integrity. When we are inclined to tell Consistency, "Leave me alone!" we find her a tenacious and faithful friend. She does not cower when our mood falters. We face days when we do not feel like thinking or acting like a Christian. Perhaps you even have memories, like mine, of thorny times when discouragement tempted you to back away from your commitment to evangelize. Consistency is that which guards us against such possible defeat. It finishes the job it begins. It enables us to competently fulfill the Great Commission one step at a time.

Consider Jesus, in heaven, before his incarnation. He was committed to coming to Earth, to living among us and to dying on a cross for our sins. Once here, as the harsh reality of crucifixion approached, his prayer proved his unwavering commitment: "Father, if you are willing, take this cup from me; yet not my will, but yours be done" (Lk 22:41). There are days when I use this prayer in evangelism, asking God whether there isn't a way out of the arduous commitment it requires but also asking for strength to face what I should not avoid.

I've found all major commitments, including the commitment to evangelize, are best kept when exercised and renewed one day at a time. I haven't yet met a person that simply woke up one morning and, after the first yawn and first cup of coffee, slipped into all the character, intention and consistency of an evangelist. Personally, I didn't start out with any "ideal" evangelizing skills or intentions, but over the years, through trial and error, I've grown very comfortable with the approach I've described in this book.

I'm compelled to be thorough because I am grieved by what happens when evangelists aren't. Unfortunately, roughly 160 million adults in America who define themselves as Christians are not committed to biblical teachings.[1] This means that many professing Christians live lives that are not appreciably different from the lives of those who profess no belief in God.

A commitment to evangelism doesn't begin when we "feel like we can do it" or even when we can say, "Oh well, I ought to try." A commitment to evangelism begins when we believe that God calls us to it (Mt 28:18-20) and that, in the Holy Spirit, God generously gives all the needed resources for our effectiveness (Acts 1:8). That said, I quickly add that evangelism is essentially an exciting task but one accompanied by peak moments and by bleak days when Satan twists our weakness and failure into a powerfully persuasive temptation to quit. My experience is that we can pray when we are gutless, weary or *whatever*. God will not fail to restore us. He does disappoint any believer who puts his faith in him (Ps 22:5).

## CONSISTENCY IN RELATIONSHIP

Years ago my friend Ken said something so seemingly simple that he was surprised when it left me speechless. I was profoundly affected by it and have never forgotten it. Ken was the top civilian employee at what was then the Pacific Missile Test Center at Point Mugu, north of Los Angeles. He was in charge of more than three thousand highly technical and highly trained employees. He was also the chairman of the board of elders at our church. He taught adult Christian education classes and for years led the high school youth group. Ken had a wealth of experience dealing with people. This is what he said: "I think the fundamental truth of Christianity and the intent of the biblical message is 'how to relate': how to relate to God and to each other." Consistency—soundness, wholeness, the absence of contradiction—is a characteristic of those who relate to others as Jesus did.

I look back and realize that until this point I had never considered that theology had anything to do with human relationships. Theology was the study of God, of his character, of his word, of what I could know about him. As I reflect, I marvel that I so easily missed that *what* God said was utterly relational. Ken's statement was a wake-up call for me.

Now I knew Ken well enough to know that his theology was solid. I also knew that he had firsthand, painful experiences with some Christians whose theology had not filtered down to the way they treated others. He was a natural and trained leader who, after forty years of working with a variety of people inside and outside the church, had distilled God's call to its essence, relationship—how God relates to us, how we relate to him, how we relate to others, how we relate to ourselves.

Peter writes, "Now that you have purified yourselves by obeying the truth so that you have sincere love for your brothers, love one another deeply, from the heart. For you have been born again, not of

perishable seed, but of imperishable, through the living and enduring word of God" (1 Pet 1:22-23). And Paul encourages us, saying,
"Let us not become weary in doing good, for at the proper time we
will reap a harvest if we do not give up. Therefore, as we have opportunity, let us do good to all people, especially to those who belong to
the family of believers" (Gal 6:9-10).

One of the privileges of being born again is that, day by day, God
is transforming us; he is making us consistent people of integrity,
able to care and love. This is the basis of evangelism.

Did I say that he is making us perfect? No, I did not. Most of us
have a door in our homes that doesn't want to open or shut easily,
that frustrates us and reminds us constantly that something is
wrong. The good news is that when we are finally weary of hearing
it creak, tugging on it or fighting against it, we fix it by putting a drop
or two of oil on the hinge or latch. Likewise, the oil of God's Spirit
repairs the parts of us that are stuck and stubborn, that resist easy access, that keep the door to consistency from being easily opened.

How, then, are we to be present? How do we learn to be deeply connected to others? How are we to be consistent, gentle and caring? God
answered those questions with the "one another" commands in the
New Testament. We can start by walking in the light of these great
guidelines as they illuminate one opportunity, one person, one situation, one day at a time. First we become aware of these commands, and
then we prayerfully practice them in our relationships. Ken was right.
Our relationship with Jesus is best shown in how we treat each other.

### "ONE ANOTHER" COMMANDS

Imagine the apostle Paul before his conversion: a young Jewish
leader who ordered the persecution and the killing of Christians.
One day he was living blamelessly under the law (Phil 3:6). The next
day, after dramatically meeting Jesus on the road to Damascus, he
discovered that his understanding concerning the law was all wrong.
He began to rethink what it meant to love God and to love others. Everything changed. Later, in the midst of dangerous missionary jour-

neys, after long hours spent making tents and teaching, Paul wrote letters of love to young Christians, often from dank and dirty prison cells, giving them instructions concerning their relationships. Paul's "one another" advice forms the nucleus of what he knew would establish bonds of love between people. It also presents us with the behavior that is consistent with Christianity. When we clothe ourselves (Eph 4:24) with these behaviors, then we are living in the integrity of what it means to be Christian. It is clear from stories of his life that Paul not only gave this advice but also followed it in his relationships, even with unbelievers.

*Greet one another.* That this command was given five times attests to its importance (Rom 16:16; 1 Cor 16:20; 2 Cor 13:12; 1 Thess 5:26; 1 Pet 5:14). That it was given generally rather than specifically is also interesting. Notice that it isn't assigned only to extroverts or to those for whom friendliness comes easily. This command is to all of us.

Sometimes the simple acts of making eye contact, smiling or extending a hand while we say *hello* can launch the adventure of evangelism. But let's be honest: in our culture, greeting is highly stylized and selective. Those of us who hope to make a difference have a public behavior pattern to overcome. On the bus, in the market, on elevators, in the classroom, at our children's sporting events—do you see many greetings beyond those exchanged between people who already know one another? Before we breeze past this command, we had better see, first, that it is a challenge and, second, that it really matters.

Most of us can reflect on an occasion when an unexpected or friendly greeting relieved our souls, made us comfortable, brought us courage. Remember that when you greet others.

*Accept one another.* Who hasn't had the experience of having been warmly greeted only to be snubbed when the greeter learns that you *(a)* belong to the wrong church, *(b)* belong to the wrong political party, *(c)* take the wrong side on moral issues, *(d)* have a prominent tattoo, *(e)* use profanity liberally, *(f)* are living with someone of the opposite sex without the benefit of marriage or *(g)* are guilty of all of the above. Usually the first sign that the warm greeting has ended and the cool reception has begun is seen in the other person's face. Their eyes dull or harden and their smile vanishes. The message is clear: "Not you. Not now."

We are to "accept one another, then, just as Christ accepted you, in order to bring praise to God" (Rom 15:7). Acceptance is fully welcoming another human being. Jesus set the example of how God welcomes us. He engaged the sinner, ate with him, talked to him, defended him, healed him and counseled him. Once it was established that Jesus had accepted the sinner, Jesus dealt with the unacceptable—sin. Change came through knowing him. Jesus did not put the cart before the horse (or, before the ox, in his case). That is, he did not ask the animal to push away what he was already pulling. This is significant to me when I remember how many things Lois accepted in me before I became a Christian. She knew only Jesus could push away the sinful things I was pulling along. Lois welcomed my distinctive personality traits, which were difficult for me to accept, with delight. She was the first person who did. It was through her acceptance of me that I came to believe that God accepted me.

*Honor one another.* Doesn't honoring one another (see Rom 12:10) naturally follow the command to accept one another? When I was my own greatest enemy, the way Lois honored me was baffling. Her dependable friendship made me dare to think that I might have some genuine value.

Picture a brick of gold on a scale. You've panned for every ounce of that valuable stuff, and now you carefully watch to see that it is properly weighed. To honor means to give another their proper weight. In its most rudimentary application it means to show respect, to appreciate someone deeply. Gold is good but what people bear—God's image—is priceless. Count on this: if you treat non-Christians with honor, you've begun cutting through any resistance they have toward meeting Jesus.

There are diet plans by the bejillions that guarantee success after "just ten days!" (or two weeks or twenty minutes). Who isn't familiar with such ridiculous claims? Honor, however, practiced for ten days, two hours or a lifetime is a no-nonsense, guaranteed route to encouraging results. No wonder we are commanded to honor one another.

*Submit to one another.* It follows, then, that in the exercise of having greeted, accepted and honored one another, we should be limber enough to submit to one another (Eph 5:21). Submission is a far cry from mindless subservience. Still, the very idea of it rankles people in a culture obsessed with individual rights. This command asks us to defer to others.

When Jesus humbled himself and washed the feet of his disciples, he demonstrated true submission (Jn 13:1-9). The text says he *knew* where he had come from and where he was going. He *loved* these followers and would love them to the end and, most importantly, he never lost sight of who he was. Submission does not obliterate significance. The Father's plan was being fulfilled. Because Jesus had such confidence and strength of being, his giving of himself to others did not diminish him in any way.

Submission is the deliberate lending of ourselves, our time, our gifts and our service to another. It is quite powerful really, and it can be done well when it is done in the power of God's Spirit. For us to submit to others, we need to remember where we come from and where we are going, that the Father's plan is worth fulfilling and that the Spirit will see us through it. Submission is not the surrender of significance but, in its finest sense, the recognition of it. Recognizing the value of another prompts us to surrender. Only God knows how much and how often we will be called on to submit to others. We know this: what we *receive* from submitting greatly outweighs the cost of doing it.

*Bear one another's burdens.* This command (Gal 6:2) directs us to come to the aid or support of another person who is overtaken in a fault. Consistency calls us to be *involved* in offering practical hope to unbelievers who are trapped in the tentacles of sin. Those who bear with the sins of unbelievers are the ones who, one day, may be used as God's cleansing agent in unbelievers' lives.

*Bear with one another.* The command to bear with one another (Col 3:13) is a first cousin to the one just mentioned. Practicing this command means being patient with the weaknesses and idiosyncrasies of our unbelieving friends. In my case, accepting my own weaknesses and idiosyncrasies helps me extend that favor to others. Only then can we bear with the uncle who finds belching for our friends entertaining, the coworker who never asks whether we would like coffee even though we nearly always inquire on his behalf, the neighbor with the crabby voice that grates like chalk gone wrong on the blackboard. I'm sure you can add to the list of behaviors we are invited to tolerate.

And God did it first. In none of these guidelines are we asked to do something that Jesus didn't do. Consistency asks us to not bypass people who may have behaviors that put us off, but instead accept these people and so bring glory to God.

*Encourage one another and build up one another.* We find this command in 1 Thessalonians 5:11. Encouragement is putting courage into someone. According to Scripture, encouragement works in the following ways: through exhortation, admonishment or teaching; through begging or entreating; through consolation or comfort. Behind all the stories in this book, some form of encouragement was used. Any way you slice it, encouragement requires our involvement in the lives of others. It implies that we have courage to give. If you look for how people need courage, and if you listen to their stories, you will not only discover marvelous qualities in them but you will see that, very often, God has already been at work in their lives. It's wonderful when we can build on what he has begun. To be consistent evangelists, we must learn to speak God's words of encouragement to our unbelieving friends.

*Do not grumble against each other.* Have you ever been in a situation where encouraging words slipped easily off someone's tongue but as soon as the encouraged one leaves, the glib giver of encouragement turns to you and says something like, "Can't that person ever *learn?*" Grumble, grumble.

Grumbling grows from an emotion of discontentment that leads to complaining against others. The process of persuading someone to commit their lives to Jesus is usually long and often quite tedious, and when it comes to fishing for people, we simply can't afford to grumble about a strong fish that fights to stay in the water. "Do not grumble!" (Jas 5:9). That's fairly clear, wouldn't you say? We must resist the temptation of complaining outwardly or inwardly about the person we hope will turn to Christ.

*Consider how to provoke one another to love and good deeds.* This command tells us what to do instead of grumbling (Heb 10:24). It's simple: pay attention to how you can prompt good deeds. *Provoke* here is not the colloquial term we often use, meaning "to bother or upset." Our children hear it often enough ("You know how that racket provokes me!"). Rather, Paul uses a word that means "to arouse feeling or action." We gain influence by understanding the thoughts of others, by reflecting with them on their life with the intention of motivating love and good deeds. Some people come to Jesus because they first tried on Christian behavior! When we carefully observe and listen to the unbelievers God brings us, he provokes the insight we need to move them toward love and good deeds.

*Live in harmony with one another.* Like consistency itself, harmony (Rom 12:16) is rooted in soundness, completeness. While consistency is free of fragmentation, harmony absorbs the fragments of life and arranges them into proper unity. Paul suggests that in the battle for harmony, pride is our greatest foe, but that with humility, harmony sings. Too often we love the idea of harmony, but God means for us to love the reality of it. He will bring people to us who challenge the ideal. He commands harmony and then places us with people who, like good wrestlers, push us outside the boundaries of our comfort zones. It isn't easy, but we should be grateful. He is stretching us, giving us an opportunity to grow.

When we're at our wits end, when we don't know exactly how to pick ourselves up or what to do next, we can utter this prayer: "Father, you are the Master Evangelist. Even here, I trust you to keep me sound, to bring together what presently seems fragmented. Please give me a creative idea I can use in this situation." With this prayer you're welcoming the opportunity to be sweet music to our dissonant world.

*Pray for one another.* The New Testament contains many injunctions to pray for one another (for example, Mt 6:9-13; Eph 6:18-20; Col 4:2-4; Heb 13:18-19; Jas 5:16). In evangelism, prayer is essential. We should pray for everything we need when we represent Jesus. We should learn to be very specific about praying for those things unbelievers need from God. We tie this command to integrity by remembering that Jesus also prayed for others. If we want to treat others as Jesus would, then we must regularly and faithfully pray for them.

In Scripture, Jesus gives us a model for praying in what we call the Lord's Prayer. The petition that brings God's will into daily life is this: "Your kingdom come, your will be done, on earth as it is in heaven" (Mt 6:10).

Let's say that Gwen, my unbelieving friend, is considering divorcing her husband, Steve. One way I might pray for her is to say, "Lord, show Gwen that applying your principles to her marriage could restore it. Help me bring your kingdom down to her by sharing how you have helped me in my marriage. Open the door for this opportunity. Prepare Gwen's heart for it." Praying through the Lord's Prayer, one subject at a time, for non-Christian friends in our lives takes only a few minutes, but is a useful model that assists us to pray specifically.

## "ONE ANOTHER" COMMANDS IN PRACTICE

One spring day as Don and I were leaving to visit our sons in San Diego, our youngest, Nathan, called asking that we bring him some strawberries from Oxnard, the "strawberry capital" of California. In the twelve years that Nathan has lived in San Diego, he's never asked us to bring him any. Curiosity led me to ask, "Why strawberries?" He explained that his boss, Sue, loved Oxnard strawberries, and he wanted her to have some. Nathan explained they had just discovered cancer in her lungs and brain. The year before, she had battled breast cancer and, after radiation and chemotherapy, thought she had fully recovered.

"This sounds pretty serious to me, Nathan. Do you want me to go with you to deliver the strawberries to Sue?" We talked about the possibility that she was dying. Nathan also shared his apprehension that bringing his mother on this visit might be a bit much for him and for Sue. Nathan knows me. He's seen me interact with people. "I'll think about it, and let you know when you get down here," he said.

Fair enough. I suspected that Nathan may well have asked for the strawberries knowing our conversation would lead to spiritual matters and what I would volunteer to do. I also thought that he might not be conscious of this. At any rate, he risked my response, and it was my job to let him decide the next step. He had no indication from Sue that she was a Christian. She was gracious, charming and honest, but she had never indicated that God was a part of her life.

Like many in his generation, Nathan avoids any semblance of organized religion. But, when the chips are down (as they surely were in Sue's case), he retreats to his spiritual roots. I know this about him, and I trusted that if God wanted me to be involved with Sue, Nathan would include me. I determined to live cheerfully with Nathan's choice.

We arrived in San Diego to find that Nathan had called Sue, set up a time to visit and said he would be bringing his mother along. As we walked from his house to hers, I candidly said, "Nate, I can sense you're nervous about this visit."

"Mother, you're so strong. Please be careful with Sue."

"There's a good possibility she is dying, Nathan. Do you trust me to let Sue determine how far our conversation goes? I will try not to embarrass you, but we're going into a serious situation where she may want some spiritual help. I need to go as far as she allows. Is that okay with you?"

To his eternal credit, Nathan gave a hesitant but courageous "yes." We walked the rest of the way to her house in silence. Sue welcomed us. Gleaming hardwood floors, orchids in bloom, a grand piano, abstract art on the wall—hers was obviously a home lived in by sophisticated people who loved life and who cherished beauty. Sue was a lovely fifty-year-old woman with a keen mind and a sharp sense of humor. She worked as a special-events director at an exclusive country club and, judging from her presence and her home, I thought she must do a fabulous job. After greeting each other and hearing her declare her delight over the strawberries, after talking music and orchids, I asked her this simple question, "What are you learning from your cancer, Sue?"

Her answer was so immediate I knew this was occupying her mind. "Well, this may sound strange, but I'm learning about spirituality." I had the distinct impression this was what Sue wanted to talk about, if I was willing to go there with her. I was. Nathan was still nervous, and I felt the tension of being faithful to two people. I remember praying for God to give us all courage for the conversation Sue wanted to have as I asked her to tell us what she was learning about spirituality.

She explained that the gravity of her illness was forcing her to think about God again. She spoke of her Catholic background, which she walked away from as a teenager. She described her thoroughly secular life and said that there was nobody she knew who could talk to her about spiritual things except one of her husband's friends. But those conversations were just a beginning, and Sue indicated that she was seeking more.

It sounded like everything she had tried thus far was loosely tied to God as a loving source. Sue was trying valiantly to think positive thoughts. She had visited some sort of New Age faith healers. She readily admitted to not knowing "spiritual" people and consequently not knowing how to get spiritual help. What she had done thus far simply didn't satisfy her growing need.

After about forty-five minutes, not wanting to tire Sue, I began to investigate where this conversation allowed me to go. "I know you don't know anything about me, Sue. Would you like me to tell you my spiritual background?" I felt it was important to establish credibility to talk about spiritual things. She indicated her eagerness to hear all about it. With that permission I explained that I had become a Christian as an adult and that I had been teaching Bible classes for almost thirty years. I told her I wrote Bible studies and regularly saw God working in the lives of people from all backgrounds and in all kinds of circumstances.

I realize that each of us will establish spiritual credibility in completely personal ways. And each of us must be able to do that. How has God made a difference in your life? What has he provided that you want others to know about? In answering these questions you clarify just what establishes your credibility to speak of God's saving power. In this instance I said to Sue, "I have seen that God is alive today and that he wants to help us. Would you like for me to pray for your healing?" She was eager for this.

With Nathan discreetly twitching, I went on to say that while God was indeed able to heal her body, he might not choose to do that. "Can I pray also for your acceptance of what God will do, Sue?" Again, she was more than willing. Then the three of us prayed together.

Sue was weak and I respected her need for rest, but there also seemed to be good rapport between us. I instantly felt a genuine love for her, accompanied by an even greater concern. I had only one thing more I needed to say in what I sincerely hoped was the first of more visits. I briefly explained that not all people claiming to have access to God were necessarily authentic. "Unfortunately, as you search for true spirituality, some people will capture your attention, often with positive words, but with no basis in fact. Some will be seeking money or have some other ulterior motive. Will you promise me, Sue, to pray before you engage in your search? Will you ask God to lead and protect you?"

Again, Sue was eager to comply. She recognized she was vulnerable, and she wanted to do the right thing. What I wondered then was, *How many people are looking for God and have no Christian willing or available to point the way?* Yes, I believe in the sovereignty of God. Yes, I know that God will bring seeking people to himself. I also know that not all Christians are spiritually willing or able to get involved in the lives of people who face desperate situations. Sue was raised in the church and she felt a loyalty to these spiritual roots. Now she needed a personal relationship with God and she felt that need acutely. She was looking for a Christian solution. Had you been an invisible guest during that first visit, you would have concluded, as I did, that Sue was waiting for a Christian to come and help her.

Before leaving I promised to get the phone number of a cancer clinic that a friend of mine found very helpful. As Sue gave me her phone number, she mentioned a desire to go to church with me sometime when I was in San Diego. Summer was rapidly approaching and while it was easy to get her the phone number I promised, it would be a few months before I could see her again. I would be traveling through most of the summer, but she knew during that time I would be praying for her.

In August I returned home and one of the first things I did was call Sue. I was eager to see her. When we talked, I learned God had not healed her and that she had accepted her probable death within a few months. I felt the burden to go to San Diego quickly, but I also knew that both distance and demands prevented my being regularly available to Sue. I needed to find a woman near her who could meet with her for spiritual support. I was familiar with a church near her home and left a brief plea for help on the answering machine, but received no response. I then called a Christian friend who lived thirty miles from Sue. He talked enthusiastically about his own church and gave me the phone number of the pastor who could help me.

That pastor was most encouraging. At first he mentioned a membership class beginning in September that he thought might be appropriate for Sue. "I'm sorry, but she is dying and may not live much past September. I don't think a new membership class is appropriate for her." We prayed together on the phone for God to show him who in his congregation might be a compassionate and wise friend for

Sue. Within a couple of days he called me to recommend Brenda, a woman whose first husband had died from cancer. She had remarried a widower whose first wife had also succumbed to cancer. The pastor had contacted her; she had prayed about helping and felt led to support Sue. Indeed, how precious is our inheritance in the saints!

When I talked to Brenda, it was like talking to an angel. She wasn't afraid of this friendship and she was willing to drive the thirty miles to Sue's home and be with her as often as she could. Now, with this support, I was ready for my own trip to San Diego.

"I would like to come see you, Sue, and I would like to talk about spiritual things. Would you like me to come?" There was a pause, and I assumed that Sue was grappling with what to do. Quietly, authoritatively she replied, "Yes. I want you to come." She again spoke about her impending death.

We set a date for Saturday, and when I arrived I saw how thoroughly she expected to die soon. Our time together was a tender experience. I invited her to attend church with me Sunday, to meet a woman who wanted to be a spiritual support to her now if she wanted it. Again, she agreed. Sue had greatly changed over the summer months. She wore a scarf on her now-bald head, but she was still lovely. What was radically different about her was that she was no longer interested in being healed; she had accepted the fact that she was dying soon. She was anxious to talk about it with me because she perceived her friends and family were uncomfortable discussing death with her. We talked about it until she was tired, and then we agreed on the time I would be at her home for church the following morning.

When I arrived Sunday morning, her husband, who was not affiliated with any religion, wasn't dressed yet for church. I had not met him before. Think about his situation: His wife was terminally ill. She was the love of his life. I was a stranger, sitting in his living room and watching him put on his socks. He had worked late the night before, hadn't slept well and was suffering from a headache. We were going to a church he had never heard of. Under those stressful circumstances, David was most hospitable and gracious. I tried to be calm and encouraging. I struggled to stay afloat in spiritually murky water.

For me the church service was wonderful. The message was substantive, the music superbly done and the people friendly. For Sue and David, it was a trip into another world. They quietly sat through all ninety minutes of it. Nothing, not even the music, was familiar to them. Imagine the courage and energy that navigating this unfamiliar territory required of them. After the service they met Brenda, and Sue agreed to have her visit. Inwardly I breathed a big sigh of relief. That part of the job I believed God intended for me was done. I felt certain that Brenda would make a genuine effort to see David and Sue.

Then David took us out for lunch. Sue began to talk about what she wanted in a memorial service. Her husband was uncomfortably quiet. I felt like we were walking on eggshells, but I encouraged Sue to talk because I knew this was good for both of them—even though it didn't "feel good" to any of us. After lunch, at her request, I promised to visit her in about three hours, after she rested.

Sue was waiting for me. She wanted to talk about God. I asked her if I could tell her my story of how I had come to know Jesus, and she said she had been waiting for me to tell her. So I told her my gospel story with an emphasis on the unfair circumstances of having alcoholic parents. After all, Sue was dying at the unfair age of fifty. I told her my apprehensions then about the future and my search to find meaning. I shared how my friend, Lois, had been a spiritual friend, much as I hoped Brenda would be for her. I explained the role of the Holy Spirit, dwelling in us when we received Jesus. "He will give you everything you will need for the dying process, Sue," I promised. All this took no more than ten minutes. Sue listened with rapt attention. Then I asked her if she would like to pray to receive Jesus.

"Yes. Can we do this right now?" she emphatically asked. I offered to lead her in a prayer and show her how to do it. Even now, remembering that Sue broke down when we came to the part of the prayer where she confessed her sin moves me. Yes, she was sophisticated and secular, but she was also sinful. She knew it. She confessed it. She begged God for forgiveness and felt the complete relief God provided.

When she finished praying, we had a long and tender conversation about what Jesus was like. I was able to share several Scriptures with her. I was sitting on the floor, she was in a chair, and we were holding hands. She expressed tearful joy and comfort. We talked about how Jesus would be with her in the dying process and how Brenda would be there too. Then Sue said something remarkable. "I'm actually thankful that I got cancer. I know that sounds strange to say, but otherwise I would just have gone on, blindly consumed with work and being preoccupied by my responsibilities at home. Now I think my dying will have more meaning than my living ever had." Such is the wonder of rebirth.

Brenda made it a point to visit Sue when she could, and Sue liked her very much. My appreciation of Brenda's efforts grew as I sensed that David wasn't entirely comfortable with her visits. He thought Brenda was just doing her "Christian duty." I could understand that David would struggle with Brenda's visits because, perhaps for the first time in his competent and successful life, he was in a position of needing the kind of help he didn't have. I never talked to Brenda about this. And whether or not she knew of David's resistance, she faithfully came, read Scripture to Sue and prayed with her.

Sue and I had one more time together before she died. We read promises in Scripture about heaven. Her death was peaceful and David's grief profound. During this time I realized I needed to visit him to share all of my last conversations with her. So it was that during the next few months, I went down to San Diego as often as I could to listen to David talk about his feelings toward the love of his life, his memories of Sue and his overwhelming loss.

When he asked, I talked about my conversations with her. I explained how much Sue loved him. I shared details of her concerns. I assured him that she was in heaven and that her assurance of salvation enabled her to die in peace. I showed him the verses we had marked in the Bible I had given her.

Still later David gathered Sue's best friends at a beach they both loved and scattered her ashes in the Pacific Ocean. David asked me to lead this gathering. I explained to their friends how Sue had come to faith in Jesus during the last months of her illness. She died looking forward to going to heaven.

David is seventy-two, and he had waited a very long time for a woman like Sue. They were together fourteen years. He also is a man for whom faith does not come easily. But through Sue's death he has begun to believe in God. His is a gradual shift from unbelief to faith—a shift that we evangelists can frustrate if we hurry the work of transition. Presently the most comfort David receives in this long grief is talking to God honestly about his needs and his questions. He can't quite make the spiritual shift to Jesus yet. In that regard, his is an unfinished story. It is up to Christians who know him to lovingly convey to him in word and action the character of God.

It is consistency that helps Christians watch for an opportunity to treat him as Jesus would. Is the faith that is talked about by the Christians he's come to know matched by the way they talk and live? Do they have integrity? Are they whole, intact? Are they unimpaired by inconsistency? He watches, as many others around us do. Now only God can draw David to Jesus. But I pray earnestly that I might demonstrate integrity toward him since I have come to love him deeply, from the heart, and want his friendship in eternity.

## INTEGRATION

Consistency is the necessary ingredient for the qualities of evangelism I have presented: being intentional, gracious, focused, pure in heart, buoyant, wise, patient, empathetic, reflective, insightful, hospitable and creative. Notice how the "one another" commands reflect these qualities. We have explored how Jesus and early followers of "the Way" lived an evangelistic lifestyle, how their daily lives demonstrated the possibility of exercising these qualities through thick or thin. Jesus said that the way we behave toward one another is a good indicator of our discipleship to him. If we are to *make disciples,* wouldn't you say being one is surely a prerequisite? Consistency requires it.

---

## ENGAGING IN DEVELOPING INTEGRITY

---

1. What strikes you as important in this chapter?

2. Since we sometimes think of consistency primarily in a moral sense, how do you respond to the idea of practicing the "one another" commands in your relationships?

3. Read 1 Thessalonians 2:1-12. Watch for indications of Paul's acting with consistency.

   a. What do you think is required of Paul to bring these people to Jesus and train them in his way of life?

   b. What can anyone endeavoring to follow Paul's example today expect to face?

   c. Match the "one another" commands with phrases from this text. What do you discover?

4. In this story of Sue and David I have illustrated the effectiveness of the "one another" commands in evangelism. Deliberately integrating these commands into our lives steers us toward integrity. Select one command that seems most important to you now. Read that command in its own scriptural context. Ask God to teach you what it means and how it applies in your relationships to both believers and nonbelievers. Practice the behavior encouraged by that particular passage until it comes naturally. Having done this, you are ready to focus on another quality. In the truest sense, this exercise aims us at the heart of consistency.

# AFTERWORD

Evangelism requires at least these four things: an ability to recognize God's leading, the skill of listening compassionately and without judgment, courage to follow God's leading, and an ability to articulate God's story in you. Hopefully, as you've read, you have engaged in "clothing yourself" with these character qualities. Maybe it is best to think of them as fabric tailored for fishing gear rather than some one-size-fits-all clothing item pulled off a hanger.

Character fabric is top-quality, made by God and plentiful enough for all. How the fabric is cut, how it clothes you, depends on the shape of your personality, the climate you influence and God's knowledge of where seams belong and where reinforcement is necessary. Once the clothes are completed and put on, you are ready for your unique place in evangelism. To demonstrate this I have one more story.

## MY TWIN SISTER

My sister Ellen and I are mirror twins, opposites in many ways. Ellen has blue eyes; mine are brown. Her bone structure is large; mine is small. She enjoys dealing with facts and figures. She loves running the family foundry. I love hearing about the foundry but would never want to work there. I enjoy working with concepts and people. (I cannot tell you the number of books I've passed on to her, memorable literature that I love. She hands them back to me with a resigned but accepting smile and the comment, "I can see why *you* liked this book.") She's an introvert, preferring to work in solitude on her computer rather than respond to a nearby television station's request to be interviewed for the nightly news. On the other hand, I'm the social sister who starts conversations with whoever happens to be around. Furthermore, Ellen hasn't seen the need to dig and scrape through the childhood we shared. I've talked freely about my experiences in recovery, and Ellen has listened graciously.

Ellen and I travel together and, invariably, when we tell someone we're twins, we get this response, "You've got to be kidding!" Yes, we share the same genetic material, but we sure don't look or act alike.

However, Ellen and I do share certain characteristics. Neither of us is a recreational shopper, so we're prone to enter a store, ask whether they have what we're looking for and, depending on the answer, either head right for the item or directly for the door. We both love dogs: she has a Dachshund, and I have a Labrador retriever. We share Christian values and we share the value of "winning lost souls" (Ellen's terminology), but we talk about our values in very different terms.

Ellen lives in the Midwest and attends a Southern Baptist church. I live in California, in an entirely different world. I attend a Presbyterian church which would be unlikely to host a "Winning Lost Souls" seminar. To her credit, however, Ellen's listened to me talk about my evangelism experiences for over thirty years. She's watched me interact with people on our many travels, and she's been influenced by what she's seen. But her cut of character from the fabric of evangelism does not resemble mine. Recently she had an experience with evangelism that reveals what can happen when, as individuals, we listen to God and courageously follow through on what he sets out for us to do.

Ellen's husband, Glen, had a relative in Iowa who died. Ellen and Glen live east of St. Louis. Shortly after hearing the news Glen said, "Ellen, I just feel like a family member from here should go to Iowa to that funeral." Ellen is president of the foundry, and it's not easy for her to drop her responsibilities at a moment's notice. But Glen has good judgment, so she figured he was right about this. The two of them packed the car and headed west.

Once they arrived at the funeral, their hearts sank. It was obvious that the relative who died wasn't involved with church and, presumably, was not with the Lord. But the family had hired a preacher to officiate the funeral and the gospel message was preached. Ellen and Glen did what they could to comfort the family and they went back to Illinois.

The family in Iowa was so impressed they had come to the funeral that the next summer one couple (Frank and Shirley) drove over to Illinois for a visit. Ellen and Glen spent time with them, enjoyed them and figured that was probably the end of their relationship. Not so. The next summer, Frank and Shirley came again and, among other things, they all got together at the park for a picnic and family reunion. When it was over, Ellen and Glen, who had arrived in separate cars, invited them to their house for iced tea. Shirley hopped in with Ellen and Glen took Frank with him. Glen turned left out of the park and Ellen, following, said, "Shirley, I don't know why Glen turned left. I'm going to take you to our house another way."

On that "other way," which was a country gravel road, they passed a new church Ellen had heard about. She started talking about it. In fact, she was downright effusive. She found herself thinking, *This isn't me. I wonder why I'm going on and on about this church!* But Ellen sensed God was leading this conversation and so felt comfortable finishing all she felt inclined to say. Then she was quiet. Shirley asked, "Ellen, do you and Glen go to church?"

"Yes, the Lord and church are the major focus of our lives."

"Well, Ellen, do you think the world is going to end soon?" Shirley asked, obviously concerned. "Everything about the world is so dangerous now, so uncertain."

Ellen understood that through it Shirley was inviting her insights. God has put Shirley in Ellen's life. He has uniquely clothed Ellen for this conversation. So Ellen began talking about the world situation and she eventually, comfortably, got to share the gospel. Ellen has taught women's Sunday school in her church for years, she's interested in biblical prophecy and she's involved in international business, so she has a fairly insightful grasp of what is happening in the world. When she presented the gospel, it was within the framework of being uncertain about the future but certain about God. Shirley held on to every word she said.

When Ellen was telling me this story, she said she was tempted to ask Shirley to pray to receive Christ right then, but she sensed that God was telling her to wait. "Wait" wasn't exactly what my sister thought God would say, so she engaged in dialogue with God even as she conversed with Shirley. She came to the conclusion that, yes, she was to wait. Then she recalled that there is a bestselling series of books presenting prophecy in a captivating fictional setting. She mentioned these books as a possible help to Shirley and saw by her expression that she was very interested. In fact, Ellen was fairly sure that had they gone by a bookstore, they would have stopped and shopped!

Ellen relayed this experience to me with awe. Here she is, an introvert, comfortable with facts and figures but *knowing* that God was showing her how make an eternal difference in a woman who, before the funeral, had been a complete stranger.

God placed Shirley in Ellen's life through grief. God opened a door through Ellen and Glen's sacrifice of time. God opened that door further through hospitality.

## REAL FOOD

The spiritual needs of people in this world are not met by superficial evangelism. Unbelievers distrust packaged approaches. They're a bit like freeze-dried food. No one wants it unless it's the only food around. If we don't know anything else, we know that in our world today there is a plethora of foods for people to choose from.

What isn't "out there" is a supply of people who take time for others, who take faith so seriously that they take up the challenge to "make disciples," who recognize that every conversation is an invitation. The challenge is to discover God's voice so he can direct you.

Embrace your story. Get to know it, get comfortable with it, get used to the fact that everything in it God can and will use. Savor what you learn. God has done a great thing in saving you the way he did, and that salvation keeps growing in you as you live for him now. Be in this world rejoicing. God's story is in you!

Evangelize as only you can. Use the principles in this book and tailor them to fit you. Ask God to develop the character qualities you have read about here. Intentionally put your personality into each one. Ellen and I are twins but our focus is not identical. She's running a business and I am working in ministry. We don't think exactly alike, we don't meet the same type of people, and we don't approach the people we meet in the same way. Nevertheless, each of us is called to identify how our vocations, our styles, our personalities, our character and our gospel stories contribute to the Great Commission.

As I listened to my sister tell about her time with Shirley, more than ever I was reminded that evangelism is not about Ellen or Shirley, Glen or Frank. *It's about God.* He lets us partner with him in this great adventure, and he makes it possible: "And God will generously provide all you need. Then you will always have everything you need and plenty left over to share with others" (2 Cor 9:8 NLT).

May it be that we live so generously in our world.

# APPENDIX

## LEADING A SMALL GROUP DISCUSSION ON *CHARACTER WITNESS*

So you're going to lead a group discussion on this book! Good for you. My hope and prayer is that the suggestions I offer will help make this a rich and wonderful experience for everyone involved. In my experiences leading and participating in small groups, I have seen again and again that a leader untrained in basic facilitating skills can quickly weaken members' interest in a small group. Conversely, the even simplest grasp of such skills can transform a small spark of interest into a fire. You want every group member to be so absorbed in content that they're loathe to have the group end and will do whatever it takes be prepared and on time. (I know it sounds incredible, but using these techniques in an evangelism class of thirty, I had a woman who was so committed to what she was learning that she refused free tickets for an all-expenses-paid trip to New York City! It can happen through you too!)

Recognizing that many small group leaders have had little training in the principles of educating adults, I've italicized some of them in this appendix.

Let's start with a simple truth before we move on to some simple skills. Here it is: it's just plain hard to talk about evangelism. And, honestly, it's even harder to do it. So pray for your group members because the plan is that they won't only talk about evangelism in your group—they're going to *do* it. This first skill should come as a relief: for maximum effectiveness, see yourself as a facilitator rather than a teacher. The book does the teaching; now you get to facilitate group interaction. *Adults learn best what they discover for themselves.* It's your job to pull that out.

So here's how you begin. Call your group members a week before the first meeting. Assign the chapter reading and remind them that they are to have answered the questions in the "Engage" section for that chapter before coming to the group meeting. It may be helpful for you to have read the first chapter prior to calling so you can mention a particular point that piqued your interest, something they can look forward to discovering in their own reading time. With kindness remind them that good discussion is built on the preparedness of each participant. Nothing will be harder on you than an unprepared group. If that should happen, perhaps it would be wise to have them use their group discussion time to read the chapter; then tackle at least the first question in the format suggested below.

If you have leadership experience, this next suggestion may well seem obvious. But experience shows us that it cannot be said too often: arrive at the group *ready* to lead. If you are at all like me, you can benefit from the reminder. "Ready" translates to "on time and prepared." Before coming to your group's meeting place, mark your questions with the approximate amount of time you expect each discussion to last. This will help you pace the conversation and begin and end your group on time. Needless to say, those you lead will appreciate your respecting the allotted time.

*Remember to demonstrate your respect for the time and effort your group members put into their preparation. Affirm each person who shares.* So many people come into small groups with gnawing fear. For many, belonging to a small group is risky. It's for this reason that I encourage small group leaders to be *generous* in their affirmation when people share.

Have you ever been made uncomfortable in a group by one or two people who monopolize the discussion while others don't venture an opinion? There's a simple solution to this common problem. *It begins when you, the leader, understand a principle of group dynamics: everyone will talk when a member of a pair; most people will actively participate in a small group of four; only the most articulate or extroverted will share in a group of five or more.*

Every "Engage" section begins with a question about what was helpful to the reader in that chapter. The primary reason for this lead-off question is that *adult learners remember what is immediately relevant to them.* This book is filled with content, and it's likely that each person will take a different slant on a chapter because each one has a different need. Adults tend to learn only what is useful to them. The initial question in each section gives group members the opportunity to identify what that is.

Another good reason for this question is that it is easily answered. Don't get me wrong—the question is simple, but a person's answer may not be! Each reader will be drawn to certain portions of the chapter by rational or emotional responses. They will intuitively connect. Their reason for that connection is what you will have the privilege of hearing, if you have established a safe and prepared group.

To get off to an energetic start, begin by introducing the topic of the chapter; then *ask your group members to form pairs and talk about the first question.* This insures that from the very beginning everyone participates. Set a time limit before the discussion begins. When members are finished, ask who would like to share their insights with the whole group. This will solidify your whole group.

Have them form new pairs regularly so that they will have opportunity to interact with as many group members as possible during the time your group meets.

If you're leading a discussion with ten or more people, I encourage you to handle all these questions in pairs or in groups no larger than four. This will have a positive effect: tendencies toward excessive shyness or excessive talking disappear in smaller groups because it is obvious that each voice is essential. Every person in your group will be engaged *(if adults aren't engaged, they don't learn).* By always calling your smaller groups back together and having those who want to then share their insights with the whole group, you will build cohesiveness.

What happens if people balk at being in pairs or small groups of four? I have friends who still moan when I suggest such a move. I encourage you to listen to their concerns with sensitivity but stick with the format. After two or three weeks you're likely to get a *thank you* from even the most reluctant as they discover that being engaged in learning can be invigorating and rewarding.

If you are using this book in a Sunday school class setting and time permits you to add some formal teaching, I suggest you study more in depth a Bible text found in the chapter or "Engage" section. Still, I strongly recommend that you keep teaching limited to ten minutes. Remember, *adults learn best from a dialogue with their peers.* Allow the teaching to enliven and deepen discussion.

One of my students in Kyrgyzstan was a teacher who was using a variation of this method with his students. He was training teachers who would teach discipleship principles through Internet courses. The scope of what he was teaching was immense, and the men and women of his class are members of a culture not accustomed to personal responsibility. The night before his first class he was overcome by misgivings. He was afraid his students wouldn't grasp the short bursts of content. He was afraid the discussions wouldn't happen. But he was being graded on using the dialogue method, so he had to follow through.

What happened was more amazing than anything he might have dreamed. The students understood what he was communicating and they worked out the problems of distance learning together. Not only did they have fabulous ideas, but they took ownership of what they were being taught by enthusiastically committing to the work.

You can make this happen with two tools: this book and your commitment to engaging your members in dialogue.

# NOTES

## CHAPTER 1: INTENTIONAL

[1]George Barna, *Re-churching the Unchurched* (Ventura, Calif.: Issachar Resources, 2000), p. 15. For Barna's research, the "unchurched" included people who have not attended church, except for weddings and funerals, in six months.

[2]"American Faith Is Diverse, as Shown Among Five Faith-Based Segments," Barna Research Online (January 29, 2002), <www.barna.org/cgi-bin/Page-PressRelease.asp?PressReleaseID=105&Reference=C>.

[3]Lance Armstrong, *It's Not About the Bike* (New York: Berkley Books, 2001), pp. 112-13.

## CHAPTER 2: GRACIOUS

[1]J. I. Packer, *Evangelism and the Sovereignty of God* (Downers Grove, Ill.: InterVarsity Press, 1961), pp. 37-38.

[2]Gerald G. May, *Will and Spirit: A Contemplative Psychology* (San Francisco: HarperSanFrancisco, 1982), pp. 70-71.

[3]Robert I. Fitzhenry, ed., *Barnes and Noble Book of Quotations* (New York: Barnes & Noble, 1981), p. 33.

[4]Kathleen Norris, *Amazing Grace: A Vocabulary of Grace* (New York: Riverhead, 1998), pp. 150-51.

## CHAPTER 3: FOCUSED

[1]Richard J. Leider and David A. Shapiro, *Whistle While You Work* (San Francisco: Berrett-Koehler, 2001), p. 50.

[2]Ibid., p. 7.

[3]Alfred Armand Montapert, ed., *Distilled Wisdom* (Los Angeles: Books of Value, 1964), p. 70.

## CHAPTER 4: PURE IN HEART

[1]Richard Wurmbrand, *Sermons in Solitary Confinement* (London: Hodder & Stoughton, 1969), p. 7.

[2]Frederick Buechner, *The Clown in the Belfry* (San Francisco: HarperCollins, 1992), p. 91.

[3]Ibid., p. 99.

[4]Ibid., p. 103.

## CHAPTER 5: BUOYANT

[1]Thomas Cahill, *Desire of the Everlasting Hills: The World Before and After Jesus* (New York: Anchor, 1999), p. 228.

## CHAPTER 6: WISE

[1]For an in-depth application of fishing to discipleship and evangelism, see Jim Grassi, *Promising Waters: Stories of Fishing and Following* (Eugene, Ore.: Harvest House, 1996).

[2]Mendel Nun, *The Sea of Galilee and Its Fishermen in the New Testament* (Israel: Kibbutz Ein Gev, 1989), pp. 17-18.

[3]Dallas Willard, *Spirit of the Disciplines* (San Francisco: Harper & Row, 1988), p. 8.

[4]E. M. Blaiklock, "Roman Religion," in *The Zondervan Pictorial Encyclopedia of the Bible*, ed. Merrill C. Tenney (Grand Rapids, Mich.: Zondervan, 1976), 5:148.

[5]George Barna's research reveals that only 8 percent of Americans choose a religion other than Christianity.

[6]John Drane, *Evangelism for a New Age* (London: Marshall Pickering, 1994), p. 92.

## CHAPTER 7: PATIENT

[1]Emory A. Griffin, *The Mind Changers: The Art of Christian Persuasion* (Wheaton, Ill.: Tyndale House, 1976), p. 28.

[2]Ibid.

[3]Kenneth Leech, *True Prayer* (San Francisco: HarperSanFrancisco, 1980), p. 127.

[4]Griffin, *Mind Changers*, pp. 129-30. The titles are his, the commentary is mine.

## CHAPTER 8: EMPATHETIC

[1]M. Scott Peck, *The Road Less Traveled* (New York: Touchstone, 1978), pp. 121-22.

[2]Tony Castle, compiler, *The New Book of Christian Quotations* (New York: Crossroads, 1984), p. 253.

[3]Eugene H. Peterson, *Five Smooth Stones for Pastoral Work* (Grand Rapids, Mich.: Eerdmans, 1980), pp. 28-29.

[4]Castle, *New Book,* p. 12.

## CHAPTER 9: REFLECTIVE

[1]Tony Castle, compiler, *The New Book of Christian Quotations* (New York: Crossroads, 1984), p. 138.

## CHAPTER 10: INSIGHTFUL

[1]Compare Luke 2:52 with Matthew 12:25; Luke 6:8; and John 1:47-48; 2:24-25. You will discover that the increase in Jesus' insight came during the years from age twelve to when he began his public ministry.

[2]David W. Henderson, *Culture Shift: Communicating God's Truth to Our Changing World* (Grand Rapids, Mich.: Baker, 1998), pp. 224-25.

[3]Ibid., p. 224.

## CHAPTER 11: HOSPITABLE

[1]Robert K. Barnhart, "Hospital/hospitality," *The Barnhart Concise Dictionary of Etymology* (New York: HarperCollins, 1995), p. 361.

[2]The two silver coins, or two *denarii,* constituted the usual day's wage for a laborer.

## CHAPTER 12: CREATIVE

[1]Dallas Willard, *The Divine Conspiracy* (San Francisco: HarperSanFrancisco, 1998), p. 62.

## CHAPTER 13: CONSISTENT

[1]"American Faith Is Diverse, as Shown Among Five Faith-Based Segments," Barna Research Online (January 29, 2002), <www.barna.org/cgi-bin/PagePressRelease.asp?PressReleaseID=105&Reference=C>.

Christine Wood is an author and speaker in Ventura, California. She has been a teaching leader with Bible Study Fellowship and is currently developing Life Design curriculum. She has five Bible study guides—*Experiencing Hope, Transforming Dialogue, Growing into Greatness, Parts 1 and 2, Yes to the Best* and *Logging On to Courage.Calm*—available through her website. You will find a link to Christine's website on the author page for *Character Witness* at <www.ivpress.com>.